People and Place

HEINEMANN GEOGRAPHY *for* **AVERY HILL**

SECOND EDITION

Gary Cambers • Stuart Currie

Heinemann

Heinemann Educational Publishers
Halley Court, Jordan Hill, Oxford OX2 8EJ
a division of Reed Educational & Professional Publishing Ltd

OXFORD MELBOURNE AUCKLAND JOHANNESBURG BLANTYRE
GABORONE IBADAN PORTSMOUTH NH (USA) CHICAGO

First edition published 1998
Second edition published 2001

05 04 03 02 01
10 9 8 7 6 5 4 3 2 1

British Library Cataloguing in Publication Data
A catalogue record for this book is available from the British Library

ISBN 0 435 354086

Typeset and designed by The Wooden Ark, Leeds
Printed and bound in Spain by Edelvives

Acknowledgements

The publishers would like to thank the following for permission to reproduce copyright material.

Maps and extracts

p. 9C 'I am my brother's keeper' from *Gimme Shelter* (1991) by Michael Rosen, *The Big Issue*, Shelter; p. 10B Leicester City Council; p. 13E, F and G Braunstone Community Association, National New Deal for Communities Pathfinder; p. 14A and B, p. 15C, D and E Leicester City Challenge; p.19E *Leicester Mercury*, 12 August 2000; p. 22E *The Times*, 13 August 1999; p. 23G *Globetrotter – Goa and Bombay*, New Holland Publishers; pp. 24B, 25D and E, 26, 27 *The New Internationalist;* p. 33C Map reproduced from Ordnance Survey mapping with permission of the Controller of Her Majesty's Stationery Office. Crown Copyright, Licence no. 398020; pp. 34A, B, 35E Cardiff Harbour Authority; p. 37D and E Lincoln Safer Cities Project, Lincoln City Council; p. 40B from *Disability, Space and Society* by Rob Kitchin, Geographical Association; p. 47B *The Times*, 26 January 2001; p. 47E and C 'Myths about asylum in the UK', reproduced from Oxfam website (www.oxfam.org.uk) with permission of Oxfam publishing, 274 Banbury Rd, Oxford OX2 7DZ; p. 48A Map reproduced from Ordnance Survey mapping with permission of the Controller of Her Majesty's Stationery Office. Crown Copyright; p. 49E and F The National Trust for Scotland; p. 51E *The Observer* 8 March 1998; p. 52A The Countryside Agency; p. 52C *The Observer* 26 May 1996; p.60A Map reproduced from Ordnance Survey mapping with permission of the Controller of Her Majesty's Stationery Office. Crown Copyright.

Photographs

The cover photograph shows Mumbai (Bombay), India. Note the contrast between the modern skyline and the slums in the foreground.

p.4 Science Photo Library; p.5 Robert Harding Picture Library; p.7E Peter Ginter/Impact Photos; p.8 both Emma Cambers; p.9 top left Emma Cambers; p.9 top right Emma Cambers; p.9D left Emma Cambers; p.9D right Strip4 Shelter; p.11D A. Broadfield, Leicester As It Was, 5th imp, Hendon Publishing Company, 1984: plate 46; p.12A Gary Cambers; p.13E both The New Deal Centre, Braunstone; p.14A RaabKarcher Timber Merchants, Leicester; p.15 Gary Cambers; p.16B David Harris/Leicester City Council; p.17D Gary Cambers; p.17G both The Leicester Mercury; p.18A Gary Cambers; p.18B NRCS; p.19F,G Gary Cambers; p.20 all Gary Cambers; p.21 Gary Cambers; p.23 TRIP/H. Rogers; p.24A top Format/Maggie Murray; p.24A bottom Sondeep Shanker; p.28B Leicester Records Office; p.28C Gary Cambers; p.29E Hutchison Library; p.29F Mark Edwards/Still Pictures; p.30A both Gary Cambers; p.31 ASK MAGS; p.32B Butetown History and Arts Centre; p.33D David Owen; p.34C David Owen; p.34D top TRIP/Art Directors; p.34D bottom Cardiff Bay Development Corporation; p.36A Impact Photos/Simon Shepherd; p.37 left Lincoln City Council; p.37 top right Lincoln City Football Club; p.37 bottom right Lincoln Echo; p.38B SCOPE; p.38C SCOPE; p.39D left Collections/Liz Stares; p.39D right Heinemann Educational; p.40A Stuart Currie; p.41 Science Photo Library/PL/M.Sat Ltd; p.42C Panos Pictures/Jeremy Horner; p.42D Panos Pictures/ Trygve Bolstad; p.43F left David Nells/Link Picture Library; p.43F middle Dinodia/Link Picture Library; p.43F right Images of India/LINK picture library; p.45C top left PanosPictures; p.45C bottom left Glenn Edwards/Panos; p.45C top right Barbara Klass/Panos; p.45C bottom right N.Cooper and J. Hammond/Panos; p.46A top Getty Images; p.46A bottom AMAR (Assisting Marsh Arabs and Refugees); p.47F Rex Features/Nils Jorgensen; p.48B David Quine from St Kilda Revisited, Downland Press, 1982; p.49E National Trust for Scotland; p.50A Scottish Highland Photo Library; p.50B Chris Honeywell/Collections; p.51c Western Isle Enterprise; p.53F London Aerial Photolibrary; p.53G Roger Scruton; p.54-55 Airpic; p.57F Gary Cambers; p.58B Cumbrian Library/Geoff Barry; p.58C Roger Scruton; p.59F top Gary Cambers; p.59F bottom The Mountain Goat; p.60 Camera on Crags; p.61C all Gary Cambers.

The publishers have made every effort to trace the copyright holders, but if they have inadvertently overlooked any, they will be pleased to make the necessary arrangements at the first opportunity.

Contents

1 Inequalities in urban areas

1.1	Different people in different places	6
1.2	Access to housing and services varies	8
1.3	All cities have a past	10
1.4	Life on the edge	12
1.5	An inner city challenge	14
1.6	Pile them high, rent them cheap	16
1.7	Home to the leafy suburbs	18
1.8	A slice of services	20
1.9	Urban areas are growing	22
1.10	A kind of living?	24
1.11	Mixed fortunes	26
1.12	Two cities compared	28
Assignment 1: Communities can change services		30

2 Changing the urban environment

2.1	Change in Cardiff Bay	32
2.2	Changing Cardiff for the better?	34
2.3	Safety in cities	36
2.4	A question of attitude	38
Assignment 2: Disability – mapping access		40

3 Urban-rural interaction

3.1	Moving into cities	42
3.2	Developing the countryside	44
3.3	People on the move	46
3.4	A breath of fresh air	48
3.5	Keeping people in a difficult region	50
3.6	Who is the countryside for?	52
3.7	A village changes ...	54
3.8	... for better or worse?	56
3.9	Too many townies?	58
3.10	The Langdale valley – a place to play?	60
Assignment 3: If I had a coastline...		62

| Glossary | 63 |

Location of case studies

1 **Inequalities in urban areas**

- **1** Brazil – São Paulo
- **2** UK – Leicester
- **3** India – Mumbai (Bombay)
- **4** Mexico – Mexico City

2 **Changing the urban environment**

- **1** UK – Cardiff, Lincoln, Coventry

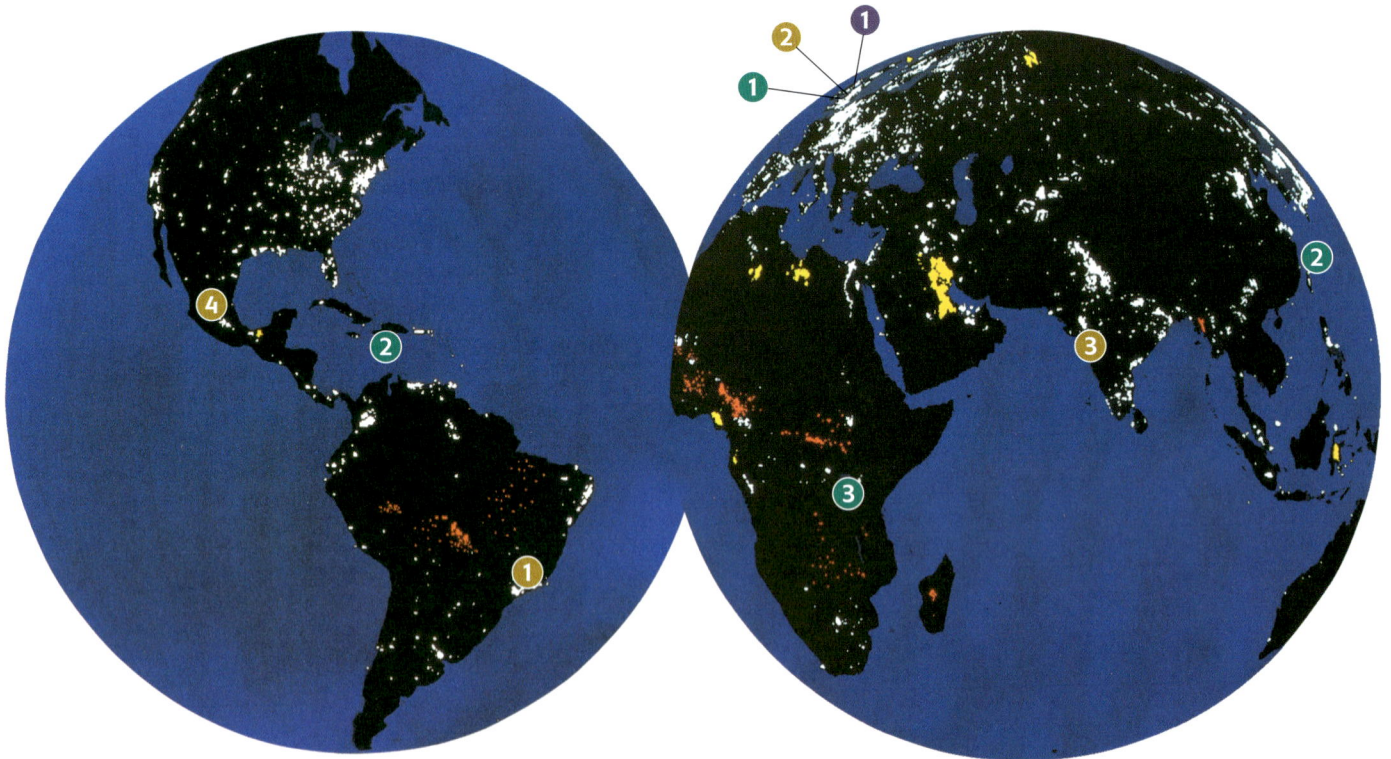

3 **Urban-rural interaction**

- **1** UK – St. Kilda, Western Isles, Leire, The Lake District
- **2** Japan - Tokyo Bay

Satellite image of the world showing areas of high population density by light pollution (white)

1

Inequalities in urban areas

Quality of life and standard of living are relative concepts.

Within contrasting urban areas there are inequalities in housing and access to housing. This leads to distinctive housing zones with distinctive groups of people living in them.

Within contrasting urban areas there are inequalities in service provision and access to services.

Housing varies in cities. Contrasts in Mumbai, India, a Less Economically Developed Country (LEDC)

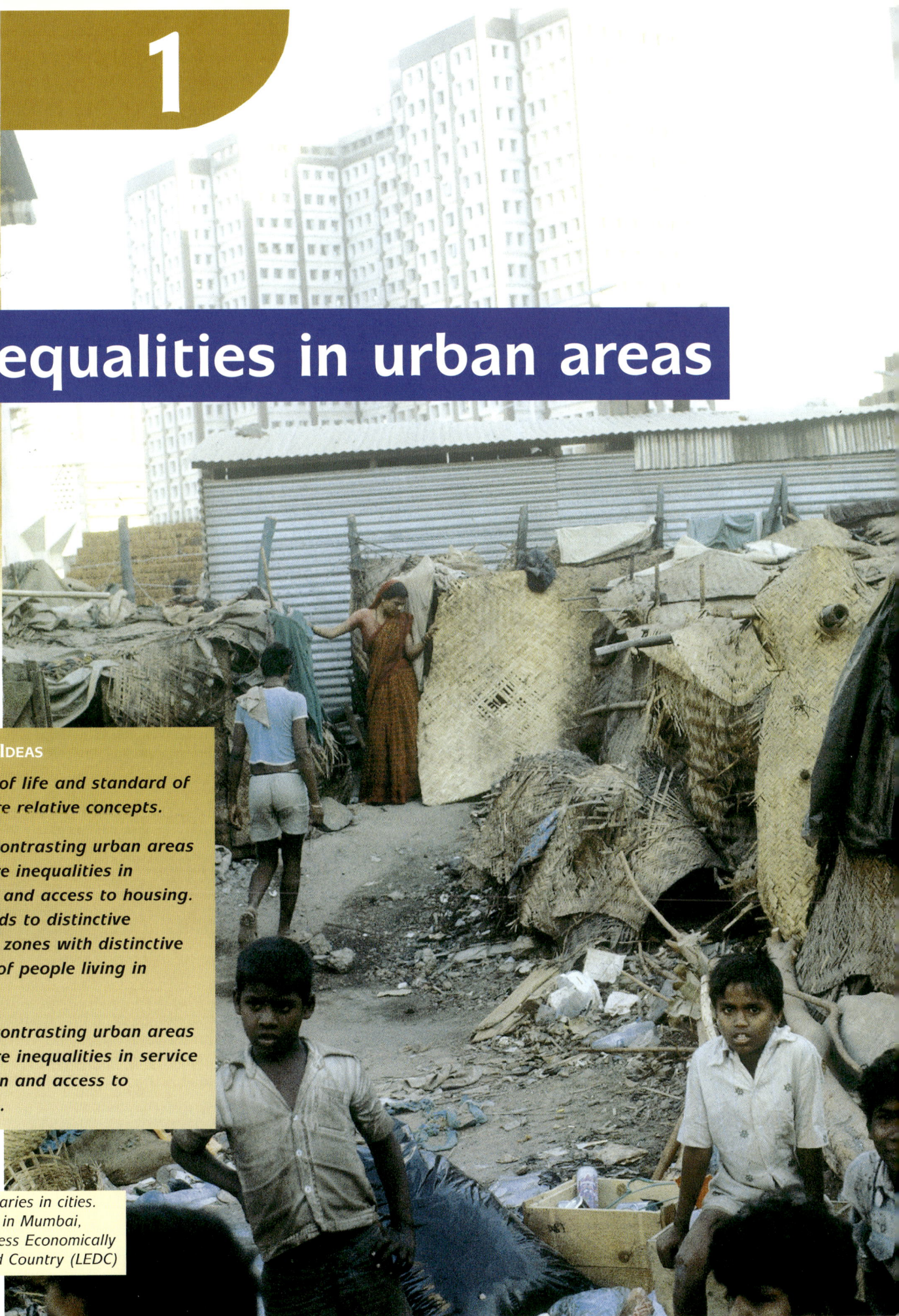

1.1 Different people in different places

Communities and neighbourhoods

Most people belong to a **community**. Many communities are based in **neighbourhoods**. How people think and feel about their neighbourhood depends largely on the different influences shown in **Source A**.

These influences also affect our **values** and **attitudes** toward the neighbourhood, and other people making up the community.

Community A group of people who live close to one another or make up a common social or cultural group, e.g. a religious community, a village community. People can belong to several different communities.

Environmental influences, e.g. housing type and condition, amount of open space, noise and air pollution.

Social influences, e.g. family, friends, links with people and organisations

A *What influences your values and attitudes?*

SOCIAL

ENVIRONMENTAL

Values and attitudes

ECONOMIC

Neighbourhood The buildings and other land uses within which the local community lives. People can only live in one neighbourhood.

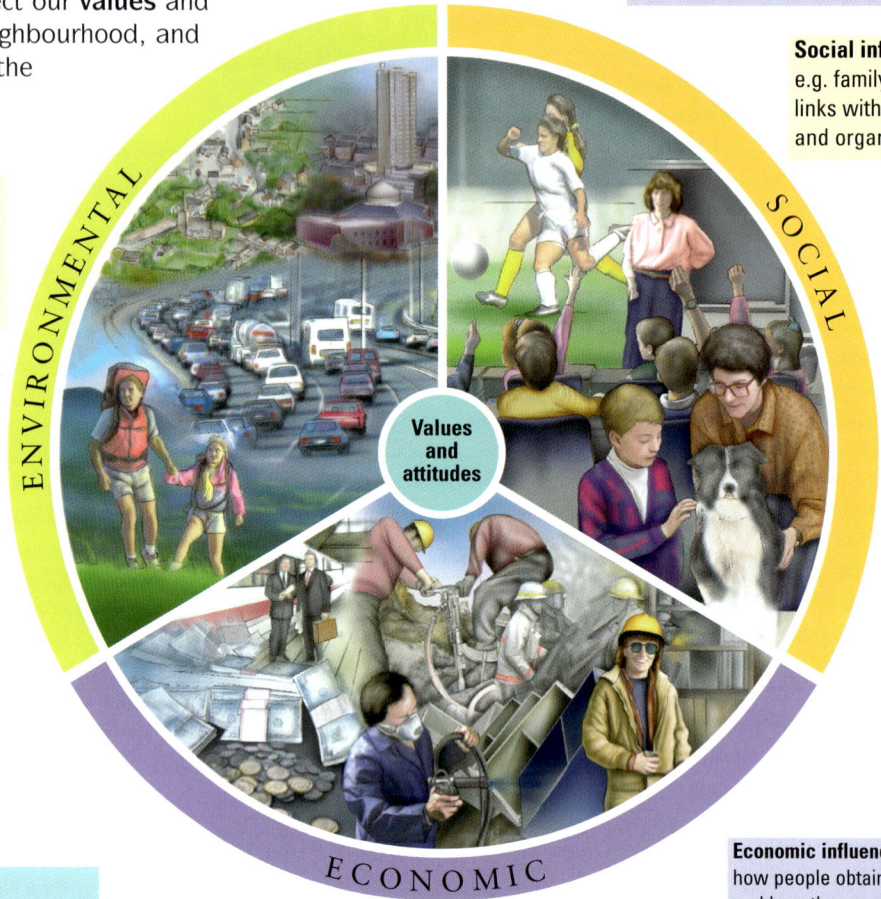

Economic influences, e.g. how people obtain money and how they spend it.

B *Neighbourhood features*

Public house	Cemetery
Sports centre	Motorway junction
Football stadium	Railway station
Religious building	Secondary school
Canal	Corner shop
Ice rink	Fish and chip shop
Youth club	Factory
Cybercafe	Bowling alley
Swimming pool	Housing for elderly
Adult education centre	Adventure playground

C *Rating scale*

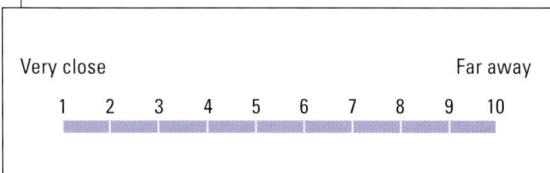

Very close   Far away

1   2   3   4   5   6   7   8   9   10

1 On an outline of **Source A** add drawings of social, environmental and economic influences that affect your values and attitudes. Use examples from your own community and neighbourhood to make your diagram personal and unique.

2 Study **Source B**.
  a Choose **four** features from this list that you would value having in your neighbourhood.
  b On an outline copy of **Source C** mark these four features to show how close you would want them to your home.
  c List the features that you would value in your neighbourhood but do not want too close to your home. Explain your answer.
  d Suggest **three** different groups of people in your neighbourhood who might disagree with your choices. How and why might their views differ?

Quality of life: *The happiness, well-being and satisfaction of a person. Among the many factors that influence quality of life are the person's family, health, income and access to services. To some people, these are more important than possessions.*

D *Quality of life and standard of living*

Standard of living: *Many measures of a person's standard of living are to do with possessions such as owning a house, a car, computers. These indicate a high standard of living but cannot guarantee a high quality of life.*

E *The De Goeses family of São Paulo, Brazil (LEDC)*

Far away places

You have looked at a community and neighbourhood you know well. What about places you have never experienced? For these we rely on other people's views. They may tell us what a place is like or we may see images that somebody has selected from newspapers, television or textbooks. This means that our **perception** of a place is based on these images rather than our own experience. Perception influences our attitudes towards other people and places, and how much we value them. We also make judgements about the **quality of life** and **standard of living** of others, based on these perceived images.

F *Comparing national statistics*

Indicators of development	Brazil	UK
Human Development Index Rank	79	10
Per capital income (US dollars)	4630	21 410
Fertility rate (number of children per woman)	2.3	1.7
Infant mortality per 1000	42	6
Population (millions)	170	59
Urban/rural divide (%)	80/20	89/11
Life expectancy: female/male (years)	71/63	80/75
Doctors per 100 000 people	134	164
Adult literacy (%)	83	98

Data from various sources

Fact file ... **The De Goeses family**

Size of household: 6

Size of house: 103 square metres. Living room, 2 bedrooms, kitchen, bathroom. Owner-occupied housing.

Working week: 50 hours (father), 'all hours' (mother).

Number of: radios 1, televisions 1, video recorders 1, cars 1. They have no computer or telephone.

Most valued possession: Statue of Virgin of Guadeloupe, other religious images.

Percentage of income spent on food: 55%
Wishes for future: Better car, better stereo, better home.

'I work as a bus driver and Maria stays at home looking after the family and the many friends who call in. The main problem here is crime and theft. We have recently installed heavy metal bars over the doors and windows. Maria always takes the children to school on the bus.'

Sebastião Alves De Goeses

3 Use **Source D** to explain the difference between the quality of life and standard of living.

4 Study **Source E**.
   a Describe the quality of life and standard of living for the De Goeses family.
   b How does this compare with your own quality of life and standard of living?

5 **Source F** shows measurable national statistics for Brazil (an LEDC) and the UK (an MEDC).
   a Choose **four** of these statistics and draw graphs to compare Brazil and the UK.
   b What do these statistics suggest about life in these two countries?

6 'National statistics are useful. They tell you about the quality of life of families and individuals in that country'.

   What is your view of this statement? Use evidence from the information on the De Goeses family and the national statistics to support your answer.

1.2 Access to housing and services varies

How does access to housing and services vary in a city in a MEDC?

How is affordable housing obtained?

Is a basic need such as housing also a basic right?

City Centre

Nineteenth century inner city terraced housing

Less than 1km from CBD

Traditional, mid-terraced house
Gas central heating
Dining room, kitchen, utility room, two bedrooms, small rear garden

Close to corner shops, laundrette, playground, schools

Owner occupier	Privately rented
To buy: £42 250	**To rent: £100 per month**

1960s inner city redevelopment of flats

1-2km from CBD

Sixth-floor flat in need of modernisation
Private door to entrance hall, lounge, kitchen, one bedroom, walk-in storage cupboard and bathroom, communal grounds
Designated parking area

Close to shops with open space around

Owner occupier	Council rented:
To buy: £24 950	**To rent: £55 per week**

Shops

Park

Central Business District → Increasing distance from the City Centre

What are basic needs?

Everybody needs water, food and shelter to survive. In MEDCs, most people enjoy more than these basic needs. Many people expect a quality of life which includes mains services such as water, sewerage and electricity supplies, as well as regular meals each day.

People also expect to buy or rent a home that provides shelter and a secure place to live. But, even in urban areas of the UK, access to housing and services varies between different groups of people. It is not always possible to live where you want or in the type of house you would like. Much depends on having a job, how much you earn and the availability of affordable housing.

B *Getting a mortgage*

'I earn about £11,000 a year plus overtime. Sally earns about £8,000 a year. We would be willing to rent to begin with. It will then be easier to move to a better house. We have saved £2,500 with the building society so may be able to get a mortgage and buy a house. But would we then be able to sell it?'

'Basically you have four choices of **housing tenure**. You can apply to rent a council house but you may have to wait for a suitable one. You can rent from a private landlord or you could join a housing association. If you want to buy a house or flat you could borrow the money for this in the form of a mortgage. If you borrow from us we will need a 5% deposit of the total price. We will then lend you up to three times the higher income plus the lower income. You must realise you will be expected to keep up repayments over 25 years even if your personal circumstances change.'

1 Study **Source A**:
a Based on the photos only, rank the **four** housing types according to your preference as a place to live. (1 = best, 4 = worst). Justify your order.
b For the housing type you would least prefer, explain your choice.

2 a Compare the location of the terraced housing with the 1970s suburban house.
b How do these different locations influence access to:
(i) the CBD (Central Business District)
(ii) large open spaces
(iii) local shops
(iv) leisure activities
(v) education?

3 Read **Source B**.
a If Mark and Sally wanted to buy the terraced house in **Source A** work out:
(i) how much money they need to save for a deposit
(ii) how much money remains to be borrowed from the building society
(iii) whether their joint income could raise this amount using the lending rules.
b Which other housing type could they consider buying as their first home?
c How would their access to the four housing types in **Source A** be changed if they chose to rent their first home?
d What advice would you give to the couple? Why?

1970s suburban housing

4km from CBD

Detached house with double-glazing.
Large lounge with fitted log fire and oak mantel, large dining room with french windows and fitted kitchen
Master bedroom with built-in furniture, two further bedrooms and bathroom
Gardens to front and rear with conservatory and a garage

Close to large park, golf course, schools, superstore and retail park

Owner occupier	Privately rented
To buy: £127 750	**To rent: £400 per month**

1950s council housing

4-5km from CBD

Gas central heating, gas fires, both close to large park, shopping parade, youth club and schools

Semi-detached end house. Hall, two rooms downstairs, kitchen, two bedrooms, garden area

Council rented
To rent: £42 per week

Extended town house renovated to high standard since purchase
Lounge, dining room, kitchen, three bedrooms, garden area, double-glazing installed, conservatory on the back

Owner occupier
To buy: £46 950

Urban rural fringe

Golf course

Increasing distance from the City Centre

But housing is not available for everyone...

There are over 104 Shelter shops in the UK
D

In 1999, the 'Strip for Shelter' day raised £250 000 for Shelter. People paid to wear their favourite soccer strip to school or work

Not everybody leaving home for whatever reason can afford decent shelter. Recent years have seen a huge number of people living on city streets in the UK. Nobody really knows how many homeless people there are. In 1999, the charity organization Shelter helped 176 000 homeless and poorly sheltered people. It estimates that there are still over two million homeless people in the UK.

'I am my brother's keeper' from Gimme Shelter (1991), compiled by Michael Rosen
C

I am my brother's keeper
Or so the Bishop says,
And life for my poor brother
Is getting worse these days.

You see him on the pavement,
You see him sleeping rough;
I usually give some silver
Is 20p enough?

Imagine when its raining;
Let's pray it doesn't freeze.
Jesus in the stable
Was better housed than these.

Yes, every year at Christmas,
The story is the same –
The homeless figures rising,
The government's to blame.

Something ought to happen;
That's very plain to see;
The problem is enormous,
Too big for you or me.

What we need is action;
It makes me quite upset.
– Pay full tax on my mortgage
Well, maybe not just yet …

4 Read **Source C**. What is the message of the poem?

5 Study **Source D**.
   a In what ways do the different activities help Shelter?
   b Suggest **two** other ways that people and organizations could help solve homelessness.

6 'Shelter's vision is of a society where every person lives in a decent, secure, and affordable home within a mixed community where they feel safe, can work and build links with others around them.' (Annual Report 2000)
Discuss your views on this statement.

1.3 All cities have a past

Different cultural groups came to Leicester

- Over 2000 years ago the celtic Coritani tribe built a village on the drier gravel bank east of the River Soar. The River Soar prevented further expansion over on the wetter flood-prone western bank.

- In 60 AD a Roman garrison was established east of the river crossing point on an important north-south road. This road became known as the Fosse Way.

- In 410 AD the Romans left and soon after Saxon tribes settled. They built the Christian church of St. Nicholas in 780 AD.

- Later, in 850 AD, the Danes invaded and the town became a fort. The now walled city of 1500 inhabitants did not expand.

- The Normans came to Leicester following the Battle of Hastings in 1066. This brought a period of peace and stability. Leicester became a medieval market town.

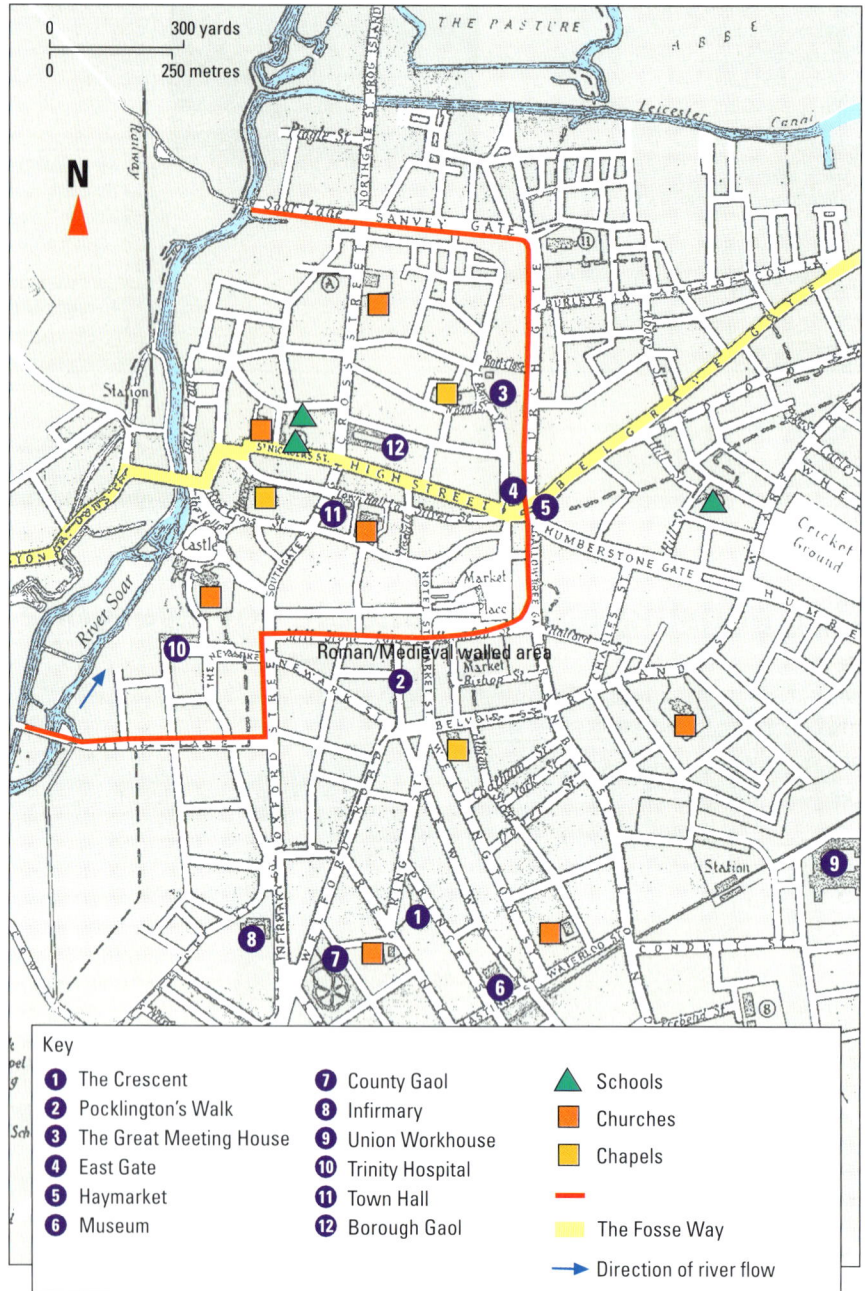

A

The City of Leicester

As you travel through any city you notice a variety of old and new buildings, transport routes and open spaces.

Leicester is no exception. The city has a long history and has attracted many people from a wide variety of cultural groups.

Key

❶ The Crescent	❼ County Gaol	▲ Schools
❷ Pocklington's Walk	❽ Infirmary	■ Churches
❸ The Great Meeting House	❾ Union Workhouse	■ Chapels
❹ East Gate	❿ Trinity Hospital	▬
❺ Haymarket	⓫ Town Hall	The Fosse Way
❻ Museum	⓬ Borough Gaol	➞ Direction of river flow

B *Leicester in 1857*

---

1 Use an atlas to:
  a describe the location of Leicester
  b give travel instructions to get to Leicester from where you live. Include distance and direction.

2 a Use **Source A** to draw a time-line from 2000 years ago. On it label important stages in Leicester's development.
  b How did the River Soar and its banks influence the early site of Leicester?

3 Study **Source B**.
  a Use the scale to estimate the area of Leicester in Medieval times.
  b Suggest the location of the town centre in 1857. Explain your choice.
  c Use evidence from the map and your own ideas to make **two** lists showing:
      (i) the jobs people might have done in 1857
      (ii) the leisure opportunities available.

C *Population change in Leicester: 1801-2001(est.)*

Year	Population (thousands)
1801	17
1821	30
1841	47
1861	68
1881	122
1901	212
1921	234
1941	No census*
1961	273
1981	280
1991	272
2001(est.)	268

*because of the Second World War

Inequality began with industrial growth

Like most UK cities, Leicester remained small until the Industrial Revolution began in the mid-eighteenth century. Most cities that grew during this period developed one main industry. In Lancashire, Manchester became the centre of the cotton industry, and Glasgow became the centre of the Clydeside shipbuilding industry in Scotland. As industry developed, some people became wealthy while others remained poor. Different communities began to live in different neighbourhoods. Not everybody could afford to live in the newer housing being built. Inequality of access to housing had begun.

4
a Use **Source C** to draw a line graph of population change from 1801 to 2001(est.)
b Identify a period of rapid population growth. Use **Source D** to suggest why population was growing rapidly.

5 Read **Source D**.
a Which main industry developed in Leicester?
b List **three** ways in which the Industrial Revolution changed this industry.
c Where did different types of housing develop? Who lived in them and why?
d What is meant by social segregation?
e Explain why access to different types of housing was now less equal.

6 Look at **Source E**.
a Estimate the area of Leicester in 2000.
b You are going to study access to housing and services in four wards along a west-east transect. Use the map and key to list their names and the age of the majority of buildings in them.

Leicester's hosiery* industry began in the early eighteenth century. Before the Industrial Revolution, knitters or hosiers worked on machines called stocking frames. These were hand-operated by men in their own cottages in surrounding villages as well as the town. Hosiers worked long hours for low wages and paid high rents for the stocking frames. The industry became very **labour-intensive** and children followed in their parents' footsteps. Families could not afford to train in other crafts.

D *Leicester – an industrial city*

With the **Industrial Revolution** came steam-powered knitting machines. These were used in large factories in Leicester, like Corah's. People migrated into the town to work in the factories. Most hosiery workers were now women as men found work in the new shoemaking and light engineering industries.

As the town prospered so different neighbourhoods grew up. Tightly packed terraced houses were built for the working classes to the west of the river in areas like Westcotes. Here the poor quality low-lying land was prone to flooding. The wealthier middle classes with access to new Leicester to London railway lines moved south into suburbs like Evington. Unlike towns before the Industrial Revolution, different classes now began to live in different areas. We call this **social segregation**. These different types of housing caused inequality of access; not everybody could afford to live where they wished.

* Hosiery is the production of knitted or woven garments such as socks and stockings.

E *The growth of Leicester*

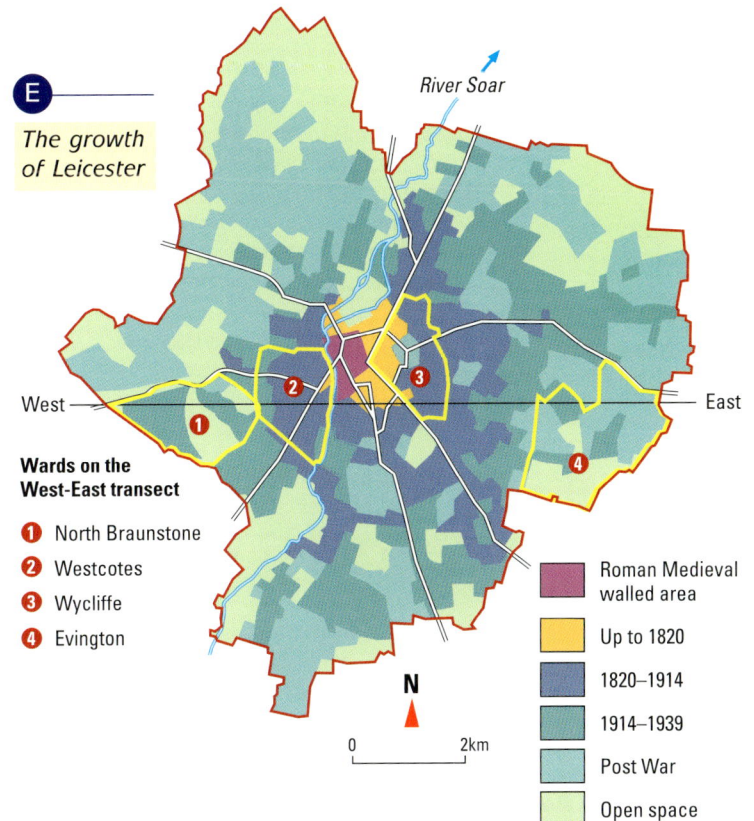

River Soar

West — East

Wards on the West-East transect

1 North Braunstone
2 Westcotes
3 Wycliffe
4 Evington

N

0 | 2km

Roman Medieval walled area
Up to 1820
1820–1914
1914–1939
Post War
Open space

1.4 Life on the edge

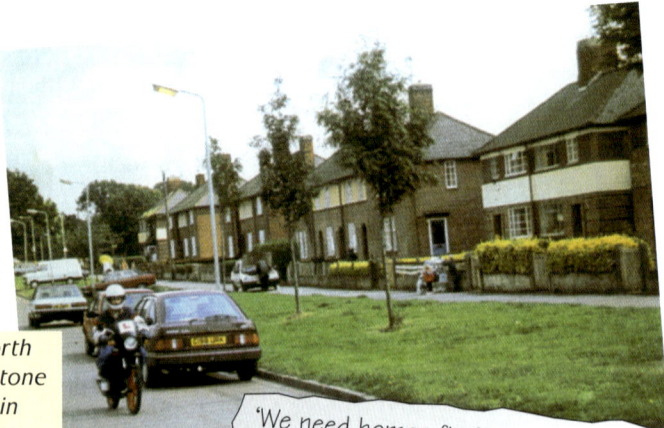

The North Braunstone Estate in Leicester

A

B 'We need homes fit for heroes, built on pleasantly laid out wide roads with ample spaces. The homes should be pleasant to live in and pleasant to look at'

Councillor Hallam 1924

New hope for the overcrowded

Council housing estates like the one in **Source A** are a familiar sight in the middle and outer **suburbs** of most UK cities. Many estates were built in the 1920s and 1930s to provide better homes for people living in crowded Victorian terraced housing in the **inner city**. These estates were built by the council to provide affordable rented accommodation.

For people crammed into unhealthy slums these appeared to be 'dream homes'. However all housing areas change over time, as do the hopes and expectations of people. The 'dream homes' of North Braunstone in the 1930s are described by many people as a 'problem estate' now. Why has the dream faded?

C *Without work it is difficult to improve the quality of life*

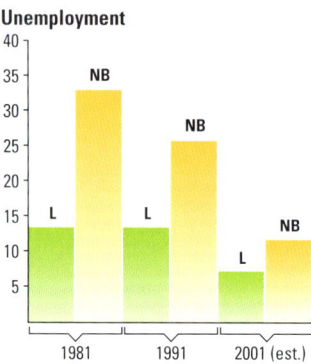

Unemployment

Figures in percentages
L = Leicester
NB = North Braunstone

Problems in getting work	Percentage listing this problem
Jobs too far away	16
No qualifications	13
Bus fare costs	12
No experience	11
Children at home	9
Too old	4
Poor health/disabled	3
Estate's reputation	3
Prison record	2

(73% of the employment survey listed problems)

Desperate mothers barter for food

AVERAGE FAMILY INCOME IS UNDER £9000 A YEAR

The only person doing well is the loan shark

If you come from North Braunstone you've got no chance. It's always been that way – ever since people were moved here from slum terraces in Wharf Street.

The Right-to-Buy scheme
A new scheme to improve access to private housing was launched by the government in 1981. This Right-to-Buy scheme allows council house tenants to buy their own homes at a low price. The discount depends on how many years tenants have rented their home.

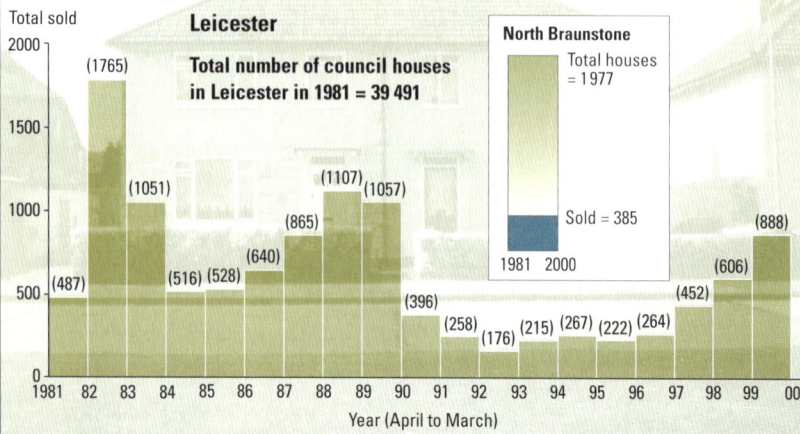

Leicester
Total number of council houses in Leicester in 1981 = 39 491

North Braunstone
Total houses = 1977
Sold = 385
1981   2000

D *Council house sales in Leicester and North Braunstone 1981-2000*

1 Read Councillor Hallam's vision in **Source B**. To what extent do you think the houses in **Source A** live up to his vision?

2 Study **Source C**.
a What was the unemployment figure for North Braunstone in 1981?
b Compare unemployment here with Leicester in 1981, 1991 and 2001 (est).
c Draw a graph showing the main problems in getting work.

3 Study **Source D**.
a In which year were most council houses sold in Leicester? Suggest why?
b What percentage of Leicester's council homes were sold between 1981 and 2000? To what extent was the scheme a success?
c What percentage of council homes were sold in North Braunstone between 1981 and 2000?
d Use evidence from **Source C** to suggest reasons for the difference in your answers to 3b and 3c.

Safety
• high crime rate especially burglary, assault, arson
• adults feel unsafe at night, at home or walking alone

Work
• only 55% of 18-24 year olds in work
• Co-op employs 40 people; few other local prospects.

The living environment
• over 120 council houses empty and boarded up
• fly-tipping in gardens and vandalism rife

Health and fitness
• highest rate of teenage pregnancies in the city
• highest mortality rates in the city especially from heart disease and lung cancer
• higher than average prescribing of anti-depressants and drugs

Educational attainment
• 84% school attendance
• 40% leave school with no GCSE grades
• 15.4% achieve 5 GCSE A*-C grades
• few childcare or after-school facilities

Community confidence and involvement
• community feels isolated; only 48% have transport and bus services poor

E *Main challenges identified in the bid for New Deal money for North Braunstone*

A New Deal for North Braunstone

Although the Right-to-Buy scheme has not been very successful on this estate, there are high hopes for a new scheme – the New Deal. In December 1999, the government awarded North Braunstone £49.5 million to improve the area over seven years. The scheme began in July 2000. Hopes are high that the estate will lose its image as the most economically-deprived in the East Midlands and the fifth worst in the UK.

4 Study **Sources C** and **E**.
  a Choose **six** problems that you think need tackling urgently to improve life on the estate.
  b Explain why you chose these.

5 The New Deal scheme has a 'Vision' as shown in **Source F**. Of what value do you think having this will be over the next 10 years?

6 Read **Source G**.
  a Write down the **six** themes of the New Deal scheme.
  b Give **one** example of a solution from each theme. Explain how each of your examples may solve a problem in **Source E**.
  c Add **one** idea of your own for each theme. Explain how your idea might solve a problem mentioned in **Source E**.

7 Produce the first front page of **The Braunstone Alert**, the new community magazine for the North Braunstone estate. You need to:
  • describe the aims of the New Deal
  • let people know how they can contribute to decision-making
  • invite different groups of people to send in their comments and ideas.
  Also include some local advertising and a competition.

F *The ten year vision*

The Vision
'Ten years from now, Braunstone will be a beautiful place to live. Local people will enjoy good quality housing, services and facilities. We will be confident, well educated and hard working.

A New Deal for BRAUNSTONE United & Confident!

We will be fit and healthy and live without the fear of crime. We will be fully involved in, and own, the process of improving our estate, and will work with others who share our vision. We will share our brighter and better Braunstone with the rest of the world.'

G *The New Deal – some ideas to meet the challenges*

Theme 1: Making Braunstone safe
• Youthwork Programmes
• police officers on the beat and CCTV

Theme 4: Making Braunstone fit and healthy
• support for parents in early years
• theatre workshops in health education

Theme 2: Making Braunstone work
• grants for small-scale enterprises on the estate
• improve image and access to bank loans and credit

Theme 5: Raising educational attainment
• breakfast clubs at schools
• introduce easy readers schemes

Theme 3: Improving the living environment
• wardens in Braunstone Park
• pocket parks

Theme 6: Making Braunstone united and confident
• an annual carnival
• community magazine and internet café
• involve the community in New Deal decisions

1.5 An inner city challenge

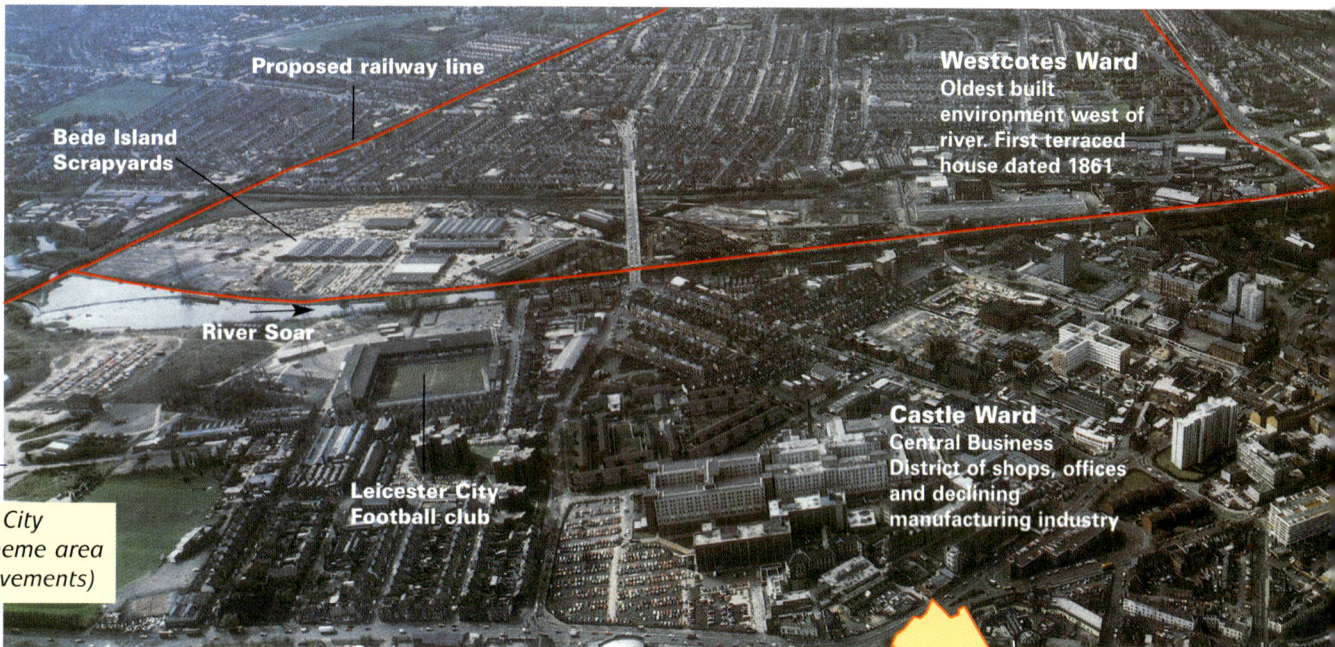

Westcotes Ward
Oldest built environment west of river. First terraced house dated 1861

Proposed railway line

Bede Island Scrapyards

River Soar

Leicester City Football club

Castle Ward
Central Business District of shops, offices and declining manufacturing industry

A

A view of the City Challenge Scheme area (before improvements)

Improving the inner city area around Westcotes

In 1992 the Westcotes area was one of the most deprived in Leicester. Unemployment was higher than Leicester's average and many houses were in need of repair. A quarter of Leicester's derelict land was in the area around the Westcotes and Castle wards.

Governments and local councils are always looking for new ways to improve the quality of life in inner city areas like Westcotes. The City Challenge Scheme was introduced by the government in 1991. It invited councils to compete for money for **urban renewal** schemes. Leicester City Council applied to the Scheme for funds and was successful in its 1992 bid. Since the introduction of the Scheme more than £165 million has been spent in the area.

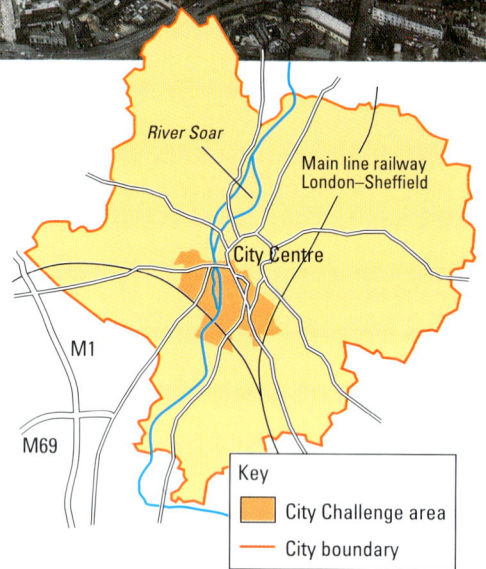

River Soar

Main line railway London–Sheffield

City Centre

M1

M69

Key

City Challenge area

City boundary

N

0   2 km

B Involving people in managing the challenge

The Chief Executive and support staff (two representatives each from both the public and private sectors and the community) monitor the City Challenge Project, control its finances and liaise with groups on the City Challenge Board.

Leicester City Challenge Board (LCCB): Chairperson

Chief executive	Public sector	Private sector	Community
	Leicestershire Health Authority	Training and Enterprise Council Chamber of Commerce Asian business groups Leicester University and De Montfort University Business Council representative	Six elected representatives, e.g. tenants and residents' associations, disabled groups, BICA (Bede Island Community Association), religious groups
	Leicester City Council		
	Leicestershire County Council		

1 a Westcotes was the first area of terraced housing to be built west of the River Soar. Look back at pages 10 and 11 to remind yourself why this area had no housing before 1861.

b Use **Source A** and the information on page 11 to describe the location of Westcotes and Castle wards.

2 Money awarded under the City Challenge Scheme was given on condition that the city council worked with other groups. Study **Source B**.

a What evidence is there that different groups are represented on the City Challenge Board?

b Why do you think decisions are shared between these groups?

C

The City Challenge Five Year Plan 1993-1998

Key: land use in 1993

- Open space
- Institutions/Community uses
- Industrial/commercial
- Derelict land
- Residential
- Public utilities
- Under-used commercial land
- Cattle market site
- Railways

Key: Planned improvements

- Housing improvements
- Traffic calming
- Nature reserve
- Marina
- Science park
- New park
- Play area
- Retail and leisure park
- New rail link
- Leisure facilities

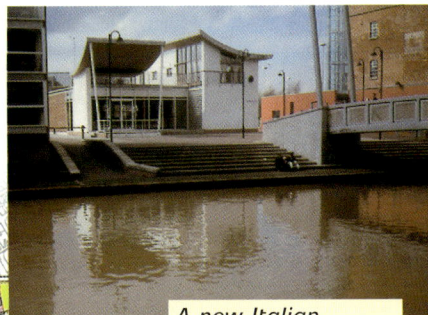

River Soar

Westcotes Ward

Castle Ward

University of Leicester

N

0   500 metres

A new Italian restaurant and flats on the waterfront

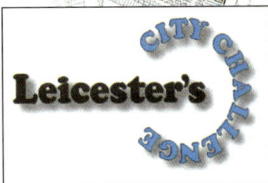

Leicester's CITY CHALLENGE

D   *Did City Challenge meet its targets?*

Targets set in 1993 for 1998

Create 2065 new jobs

Build or improve 1425 homes

Start 130 new businesses

Reduce crime

Reclaim derelict land and create green spaces

Develop community projects

Outcomes in 1998

- Almost 3000 jobs created
- Over 4000 houses built or improved
- Over 250 businesses set up
- Street lighting increased; free locks and security advice provided
- Five pocket parks plus a two hectare park created
- Projects include childcare for working parents, lunchtime clubs for elderly Asians

E   *The verdict*

'City Challenge money has enabled us to increase access to affordable housing and local services for many different groups of people. Most of our measurable targets have been achieved, but the real indicator of success is how the community feels about its area. The five-year scheme has now been replaced by money from the Single Regeneration Budget Scheme since 1998. That funding should see the plans completed.'

City Challenge spokesperson

3
a Draw and label a sketch of land use in the City Challenge area from **Source A**. Use **Source C** to help you add labels.
b Describe the location of the derelict and under-used commercial land in **Source C**.
c What different uses were planned for this land? Suggest why.
d From the map, list **three** ways in which the planned changes should improve the quality of life for different groups of people.

4 **Source D** lists some targets and outcomes of the five-year City Challenge Scheme.
a Assess its progress between 1993 and 1998.
b Explain how different groups of people will have benefited from this progress.

5 Read **Source E**.
a Why are measurable targets not the only indicator of success?
b Discuss how you would investigate how the community felt about the impact of the City Challenge Scheme in Westcotes.

15

1.6 Pile them high, rent them cheap

The future is high-rise?

In the 1960s and early 1970s a popular solution to the problems of overcrowding in inner city areas was **comprehensive redevelopment**. Large areas of nineteenth century terraced housing were demolished and replaced with tower blocks (**Source B**). The tower blocks could be built quickly using the latest technology and materials such as reinforced concrete. They provided cheap, affordable public sector housing close to the CBD.

The scheme was attractive to local councils. They thought tower blocks would improve access to better housing and the city centre for low income groups. Building tower blocks also created open space in the inner city. Within this space, planners could build small shopping precincts (**Source D**) to replace the corner shops that had been demolished. They could also use the space to build inner ring roads and retail parks.

A city of giant skyscrapers, surrounded by gardens and park land. Airless corridor streets and dark dwellings will be replaced with a sea of trees and grass and majestic crystal skyscrapers.

The city will have sunlight, fresh air and space. It is a most efficient city for living and working in; traffic separate from housing; people living in apartment blocks; recreational facilities, laundries, restaurants, shops, schools and nurseries.

A

Le Corbusier's vision of The Dream City in 1920

B Goscote House, Leicester

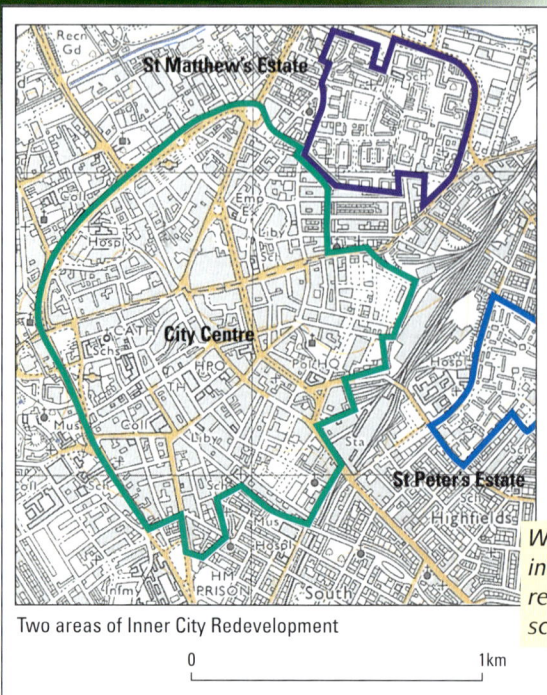

Two areas of Inner City Redevelopment

0 ———— 1km

C *Where are the inner city redevelopment schemes?*

1 Read **Source A**.
   a List **four** benefits of Le Corbusier's Dream City.
   b Would you like to live in a city like this? Explain your view.

2 Goscote House is one of five tower blocks forming the St. Peter's estate in Wycliffe ward. Study **Source B**.
   a Describe Goscote House and its surroundings.
   b To what extent does this match Le Corbusier's vision?

3 Look at **Source C**.
   a Compare the location of St. Peter's and St. Matthew's estates in relation to the city centre. Refer to direction and distance.
   b What advantages does being close to the city centre give tower block dwellers?

4 a From **Source D** list the services provided in St. Peter's precinct.
   b List **two** community groups that meet there.
   c Suggest groups of tower block tenants who might find it difficult to access the services and open space around the tower blocks. Explain your choices.

The Hilton of Highfields?

There is not much of a 'high life' in Goscote House, likened to a 'swish hotel' when it opened in 1973. One resident said living in a tower block was like being in a prison – you felt shut in. Tenants spoke of lifts that were awash with urine; of obscene graffiti; of inadequate lighting; of fights breaking out in corridors and of noisy parties at all hours.

High above the ground people feel cut off from society. A warden at the tower block said, 'It is a very lonely life here. It is amazing that you can live among all these people and still be a stranger.' He added that there were problems of vandalism and theft, and of rubbish being thrown out of windows.

Mr Derek Potter said that life in Goscote House was not all bad, 'I do not feel lonely or cut off – there is a launderette and social club here.' One woman in Goscote House told me, 'I love the view from my room and I get brilliant sunshine flooding in. I have got to know everyone on my floor and there is a real community spirit among us.'

D Tower blocks are served by shopping precincts

ST. PETERS SHOPPING PRECINCT
HIGHFIELDS YOUTH AND COMMUNITY CENTRE
HIGHFIELDS LIBRARY
ST. PETERS - STOUGHTON ST. - TENANTS ASSOCIATION
KOONER-SAVE SUPERMARKET
ISLAMABAD HALAL MEAT
CHARAK CHEMISTS
ROSIES TAKE-AWAY
ST. PETERS NEWS
ST. PETERS POST OFFICE
Leicester City Council

E Life in Goscote House in 1993

F A City Council spokesperson said...

By 1993 it was beginning to get more difficult to rent Goscote House flats out. People just refused to take them. We were aware that Leicester University had a great problem finding short-term rented property so we agreed to let them out to students. Now all the flats, apart from 20, are rented to the University. It solves a problem for them and provides us with valuable income.'

G Rowlatt's Hill 1960-2000 – Rest In Pieces

Making the best of a bad job

Goscote House was opened in 1973 on the St. Peter's estate in the Highfields area of Wycliffe ward. It is 21 storeys high and provides small and large bedsits, one- and two-bedroomed flats and a few larger flats. During the 20 years up to 1993 it became the least popular of all the high-rise blocks in Leicester.

The first two 24-storey tower blocks built in Leicester were demolished on 29 October 2000. The two blocks at Rowlatt's Hill were built in the 1960s on the edge of Leicester. They were pulled down, said the council, because not enough people wanted to live there. They had been occupied by people rehoused from inner city terraced houses that the council wanted to demolish. The space was then used to build more tower blocks close to the city centre.

5 Read **Source E**.
   a By 1993 some people no longer wished to live in Goscote House. Suggest why.
   b What good things are said about life in Goscote House?

6 Study **Sources F** and **G**.
   a Describe the **two** ways in which the tower block problem has been tackled in Leicester.
   b What are your views on these different ideas?

7 Many councils are thinking about what to do with tower blocks now that people no longer wish to live in them. Suggest some solutions that do **not** involve demolition.

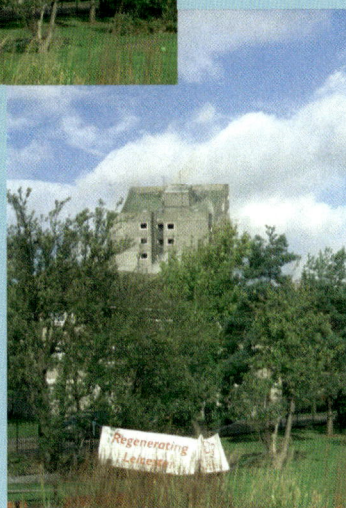

1.7 Home to the leafy suburbs

A high quality of life?

Cities such as Tokyo, Delhi, New York and Leicester are very different but they all suffer from the dreaded morning and evening **commuter** rush. Road and rail networks reach **gridlock** as thousands of commuters travel to and from work in the city centre. These people consider the extra time, money and frustration a worthwhile price to pay in order to have a high quality of life away from their workplace and the city centre. By paying to live in suburban areas they access high quality private housing and some services that are rarely available close to the city centre. In cities in MEDCs many commuters live in leafy suburbs like Evington in Leicester, near the **urban-rural fringe**.

A

Spencefield Lane, Evington

B   Aerial photo of map area in C

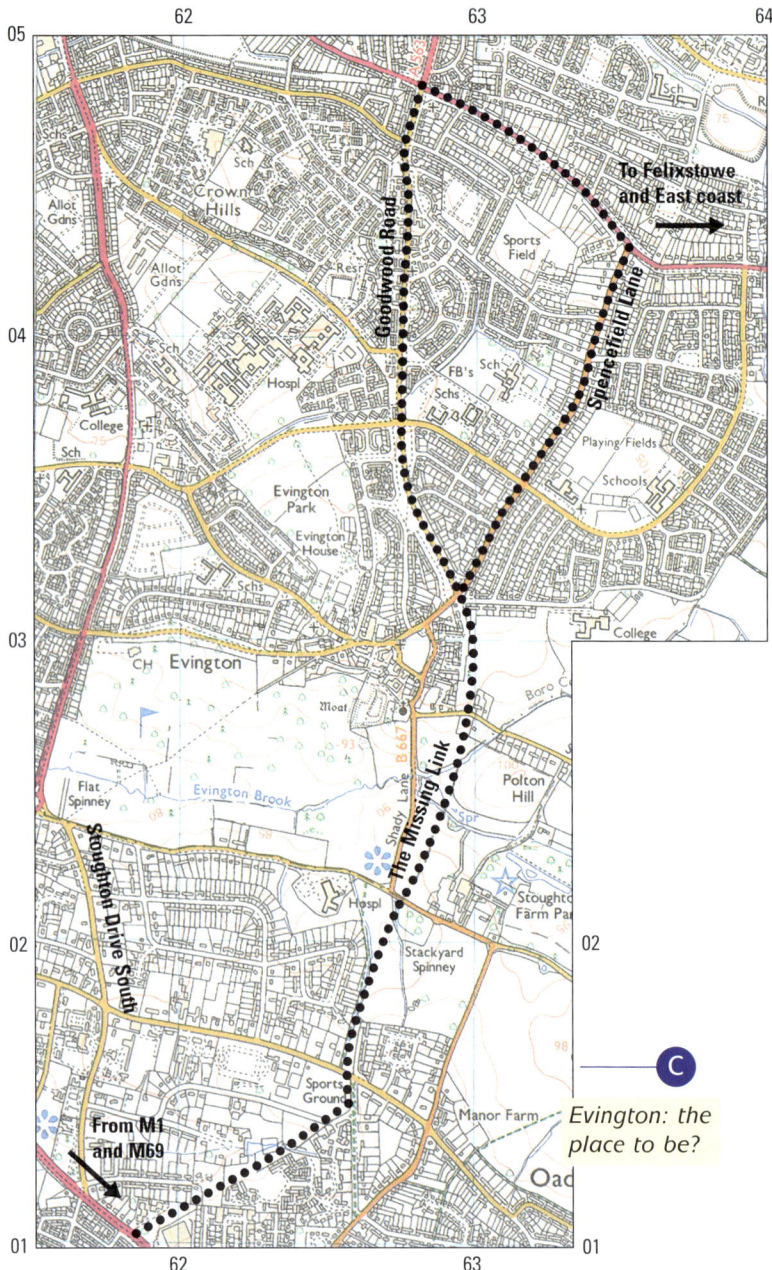

C

Evington: the place to be?

1 a List **three** features that people might find attractive about suburban homes. Use **Source A** to help.
   b Suggest any disadvantages of living in suburban areas.

2 Study **Sources B** and **C**.
   a What is at A, B, C ? Draw a sketch map to show these features. Shade them in green.
   b On your map add and shade in the following (use a different colour for each):
   - housing areas with gardens   • schools
   - roads   • allotments
   - the hospital and grounds   • other land-use
   c Suggest different groups of people who would enjoy access to the different uses of open space.

	Car ownership (%)	Employed (%)	Home ownership (%)	Central heating (%)
N. Braunstone	33	74	18	74
Westcotes	54	88	62	69
Wycliffe	28	67	17	83
Evington	71	96	76	95
LEICESTER	55	86	58	83

D   Advantage Evington?

The peace is shattered

Although people living in areas like Evington enjoy access to high quality housing and open space they are not immune to change. Increasing car ownership and lorry transport have caused a dramatic rise in Leicester's traffic. The opening of the M69 in 1976 meant that lorries travelling to east coast ports went through Leicester.

To solve the problem the county council wanted to build an Eastern District Distributor Road (EDDR) (**Source E**). This would complete the 'missing link' in Leicester's ring road. There would be a dual carriageway from the A6 in Oadby to Evington using one of three options:

Option 1 – a single carriageway along Goodwood Road
Option 2 – a dual carriageway along Goodwood Road
Option 3 – to divert traffic along Spencefield Lane.

In 1997 the council postponed the EDDR until at least 2010, stating that more money would be invested in park-and-ride schemes and public transport. This has caused enormous anger among the residents of Oadby and Evington.

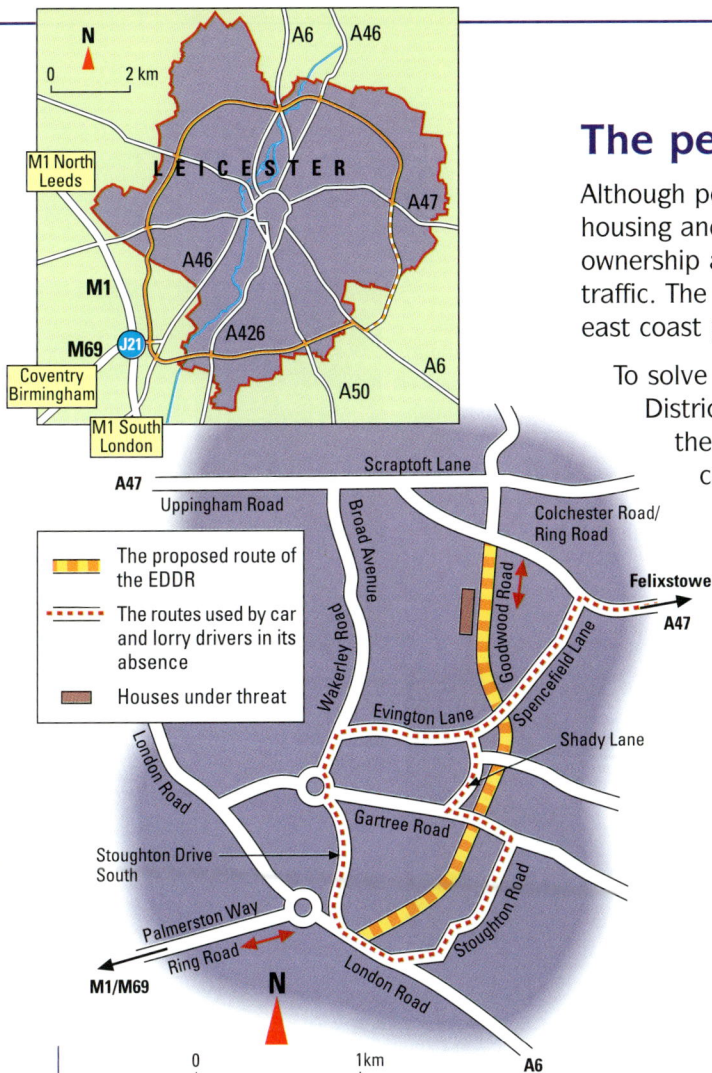

F A view from Goodwood Road, Evington

Hilda Bright lives on Goodwood Road. Her home was built when the EDDR was thought to be unnecessary. In 1996 the council said that if the EDDR went ahead it should be the dual-carriageway option through Goodwood Road. This would mean the demolition of 127 houses here. The road is already congested. "The traffic has doubled. You cannot hear the TV or the wireless. You have to shut the doors even when it is hot" says Hilda.

E A suburban issue – the 'missing link'

G A view from Spencefield Lane, Evington

'When the M69 was opened we just got a huge influx of lorries which increased every year. Since 1994 the A14 has opened south of Leicester so some lorry traffic has been taken away and the council has now passed a resolution that the EDDR will not go through Spencefield Lane. At least SPACE has won that battle but we still have heavy lorries down here bringing noise and air pollution as well as breaking up the road and causing danger to young and old. It also affects house prices. We want a ban on all heavy vehicles – they should go down Goodwood Road as planned.'

Spokesperson for SPACE: Spencefield Action Campaign for the Environment

4 Study **Source E**.
  a Draw a sketch map of the area. Label the proposed EDDR route.
  b Label Goodwood Road, Spencefield Lane and Stoughton Drive South. Add the routes used by motorists and lorries now.
  c Use **Sources B** and **C** to shade on areas of housing along each route.

5 Read the different views in **Sources F** and **G**.
  a List the effects that having no EDDR is having on the lives of people.
  b Which of the suburban areas would benefit or suffer if Option 2 is chosen for the 'missing link'?
  c Why is the problem going to continue? What is your view of the council's decision?

3 **Source D** shows four measurable indicators in the four areas you have studied.
  a How does Evington compare with the other three areas?
  b How do the areas compare with Leicester as a whole? What does this suggest about:
    • the standard of living
    • the quality of life in each area?

6 Imagine you are a resident of Spencefield Lane or Goodwood Road. Design a campaign poster that puts your point of view about 'the missing link'.

1.8 A slice of services

A walk on the west side

To carry out fieldwork for their study, a GCSE geography class went to the Narborough Road area of Leicester. This road was chosen because it leads from the **CBD** directly south-westwards through different housing types towards junction 21 of the M1 motorway. This south-west slice of Leicester contains the different shops and other services you would expect in most urban areas in the UK if you travelled out from the CBD to the rural fringe.

Small groups of students surveyed different parts of the road and mapped selected services. The result of all the groups' work was mapped and is shown in **Source A**. The students also took photographs of different shop types and were given the latest census data for the two wards along the Narborough Road (**Source B**).

Corner shops

Many nineteenth century corner shops have now closed or changed their function. Those that remain sell **low order** convenience goods such as groceries and newspapers or provide a service such as video rentals. These goods have a **low range**. People will not travel far to buy them, most walk.

Shopping parades

These often stretch along main roads where parking is available. They offer a higher order of goods and services than corner shops and centres, e.g. used furniture/carpets, banks, launderettes, clothes, restaurants. People may travel by car to these parades.

Out-of-town shopping centres

Since the mid 1970s many areas of cheap, flat land close to motorway junctions have been used for out-of-town shopping. These offer **high order** goods without the difficulties of city centre shopping. People park cars in large free car parks. Shops like Marks & Spencer run free shuttle buses from surrounding villages.

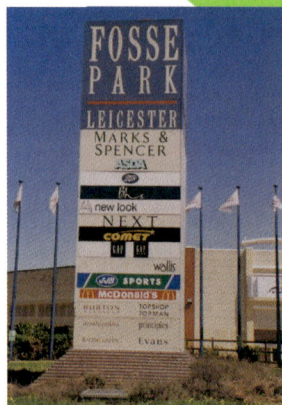

Neighbourhood shopping centres

These serve areas of private and council housing estates. The shops cluster together and offer several goods and services, e.g. TV/video repairs, fish and chip shops, post office, hairdressers, betting shop. People walk but they may also drive to these centres.

Central Business District CBD

Shops selling high order goods and services and offices are located here. Since out-of-town superstores were built the council has tried to attract people to the CBD by pedestrianisation, late-night shopping and new shopping complexes like The Shires. People travel here by car or bus from all over the county. These goods have a **high range**.

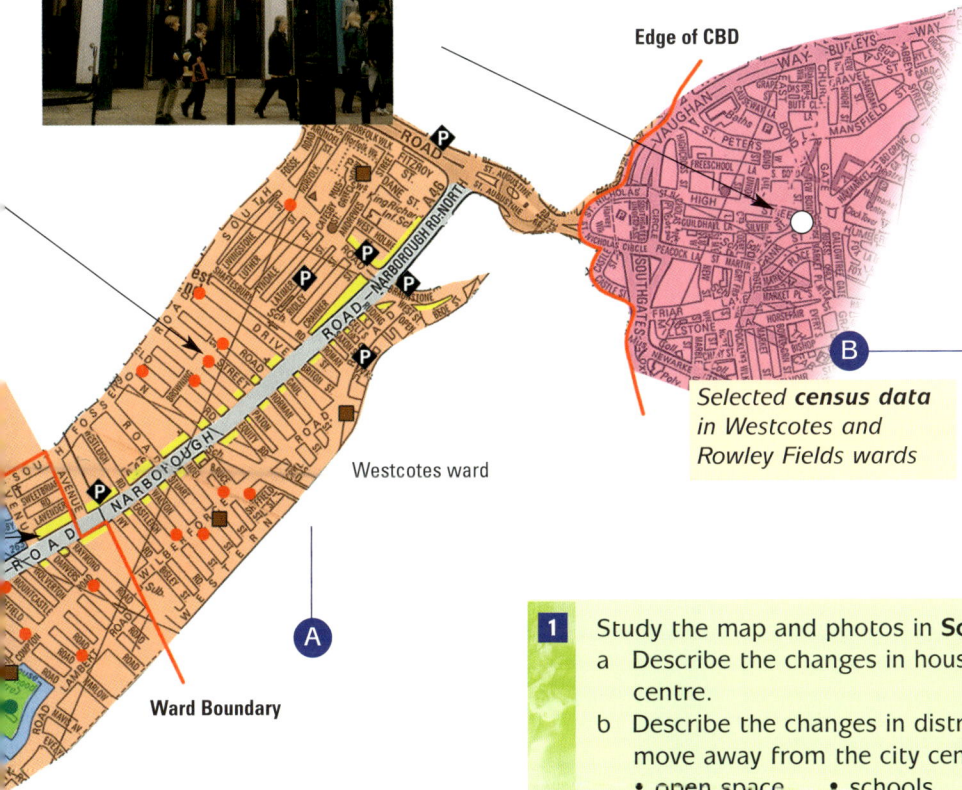

Edge of CBD

Westcotes ward

*Selected **census data** in Westcotes and Rowley Fields wards*

	Rowley Fields	Westcotes
Population 1981	10 119	9 863
Population 1991	10 079	9 622
Age structure (%)		
0-19	28	20
20-29	19	27
30-39	13	15
40-64	22	19
65 +	18	19
Ethnic composition (%)		
White	84	76
Black	1	2
Asian	13	20
Other groups	2	2
Economically inactive		
Students	367	549
Retired	1 529	1 403
Housing tenure (%)		
Owner occupiers	58	62
Privately rented	8	25
Housing Association	1	4
Council rented	33	9
Car ownership (%)		
No car	45	46
One or two cars	55	54
Household composition		
Single pensioner	641	601
One adult with children	241	122

B

Ward Boundary

A

Key

HOUSING

- 19th century terraced housing
- Council housing (Rented and owned)
- Private suburban housing (Owner-occupied)

SERVICES

Private sector services

- Central Business District (C.B.D.)
- Corner shops
- Neighbourhood shopping centres
- Shopping Parades
- Out-of-town shopping centres
- Public Houses

Public sector services

- Community and neighbourhood centres
- Open space
- Schools
- City Centre

1 Study the map and photos in **Source A**.
   a Describe the changes in housing type as you move away from the city centre.
   b Describe the changes in distribution of the following services as you move away from the city centre:
   • open space   • schools   • public houses   • shops.

2 Refer to **Source A** and the census data in **Source B**.
   a Describe the services available in the area of Westcotes ward.
   b To what extent do these services cater for different groups of people living there?
   c How do the Rowley Fields services compare with Westcotes?
   d Do the people living in the Rowley Fields area have adequate services? Justify your view.

3 Out-of-town shopping centres have changed access to shopping.
   a Suggest groups of people from the housing areas in **Source A** who may have benefited from these. Explain why.
   b Which groups of people may not have benefited? Explain why.

4 In this piece of fieldwork the students used:
   (i) an A-Z street atlas of Leicester published in 1992
   (ii) the latest selected census data from 1991.
   They only mapped selected services requested by their teacher so, for example, religious buildings or banks were not mapped. They also did not survey areas that were outside the slice shown in **Source A**.
   a Do you think this makes any difference to the validity of your previous answers? Explain your view.
   b Suggest how the fieldwork could have been carried out to give a better study of service provision for different groups of people living in these different housing types.

1.9 Urban areas are growing

Where and why is rapid population growth taking place?
How is this growth affecting India?

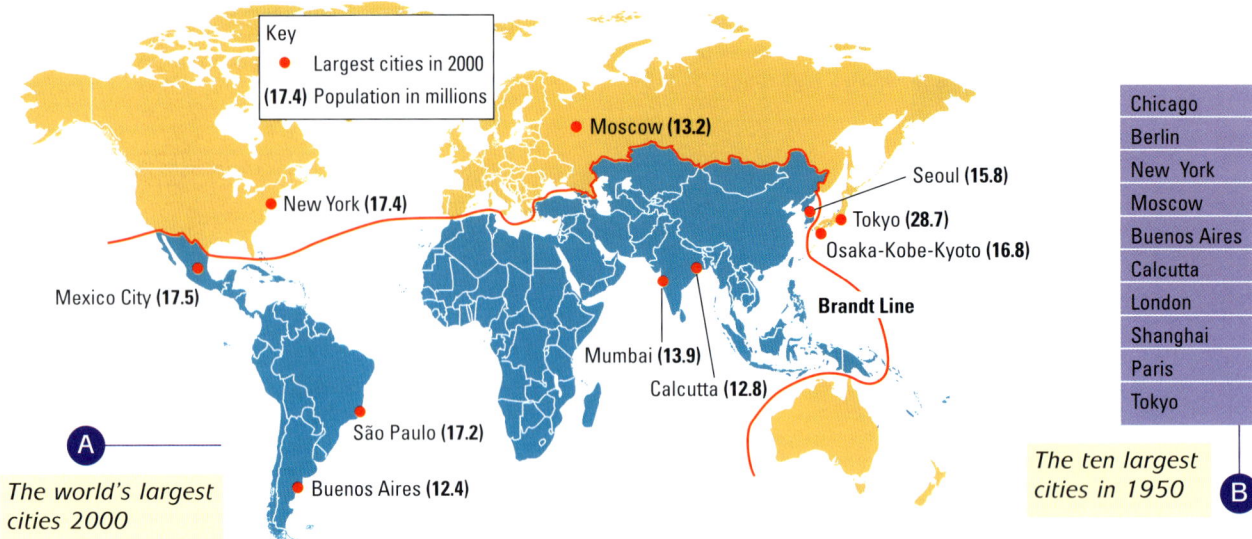

The world's largest cities 2000

A

Chicago
Berlin
New York
Moscow
Buenos Aires
Calcutta
London
Shanghai
Paris
Tokyo

The ten largest cities in 1950

B

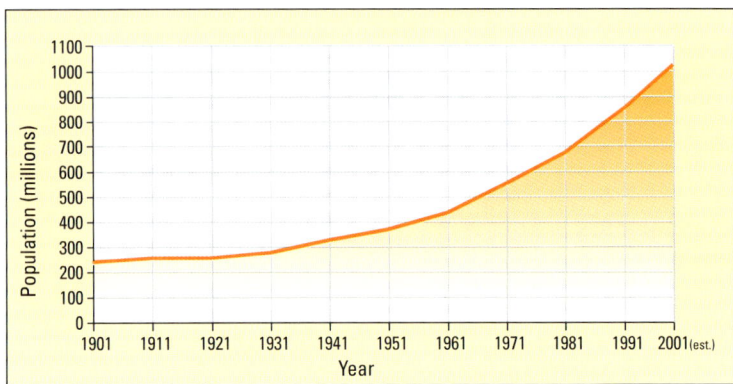

C *A century of change in India's population*

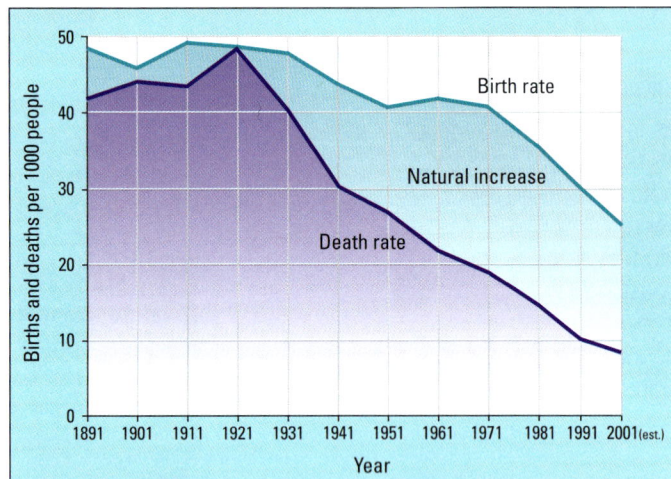

D *Birth rates and death rates in India*

Global population growth

The world's population is growing. Most of this increase is taking place in LEDCs. The growth is due to falling death rates and relatively high birth rates. These are taking place because of:

- the wish to have large families to compensate for expected high **infant mortality**
- the need for large families to work on the land in rural areas
- religious objections to birth control
- better medical care keeping people alive longer.

INDIAN BIRTHS SET TO BURST BILLION BARRIER

From David Orr in Delhi

India is on the verge of reaching the one billion* population mark. The nation, which each year adds more people to the world than any other, will officially top one billion by this weekend according to the **United Nations**. Only China, with 1.248 billion, has more people but India is catching up fast. Projections indicate that India will have overtaken China in the next four decades.

Adapted from *The Times*, 13 August 1999   *1 billion = 1000 million

E

---

1 a Describe the distribution of the ten largest cities on **Source A** in the year 2000.
   b Compare this with the cities listed in **Source B**.
   c Suggest reasons for the differences you have identified.

2 Study **Source C**.
   a Describe how India's population has changed between 1901 and 2001 (est.).

   b Use **Source D** and other information on this page to give reasons for the changes you have described.

3 Read **Source E**.
   a Describe the significance of *this* August 1999 weekend for India.
   b What is likely to happen to India's population total in the first half of the twenty-first century?

F *The twentieth-century growth of the city of Mumbai*

1901	0.8
1911	1.1
1921	1.2
1931	1.3
1941	1.7
1951	2.9
1961	4.1
1971	5.9
1981	8.2
1991	9.9
2001(est)	13.9

Figures to nearest millions

G *Where is Mumbai?*

Mumbai beaches
Juhu, 20km north of central Mumbai and close to Santa Cruz airport, is Mumbai's beach suburb, with a number of large hotels. Marve, on the same coast but a further 20km north, is less built-up.
Take note: Mumbai's beaches are unsafe for swimmers during the monsoon rainy season.

Growing cities

India was a **colony** of the British Empire in the period before gaining its independence in 1947. Many of its urban areas were developed as ports to import and export goods. These attracted migrants to them for work and today many of India's coastal cities continue to play important roles as ports for the country. Mumbai (formerly Bombay) is one of these cities.

H *Mumbai – a place to visit?*

Mumbai	J	F	M	A	M	J	J	A	S	O	N	D
Average temp. (°C)	24	25	27	28	30	29	27	27	27	28	27	26
Hours of sun daily	12	12	12	12	8	4	3	4	6	8	10	12
Days of rainfall	1	1	1	1	5	30	30	30	20	10	5	1
Rainfall (mm)	2	1	1	3	16	520	710	439	297	88	21	2

The CBD at night

Boom town
Mumbai, now a sprawling **metropolis** of more than thirteen million people, is one of India's newer cities. Until the mid-nineteenth century it was less important to the British than their bases at Madras and Calcutta, but by the 1850s it had become a boom town becoming India's most important financial and commercial centre.

Shopping
Shopping in Mumbai is interesting, with lots of antique and craft shops selling items from all over India. Silk sari lengths... modern and antique paintings and carvings, silver jewellery, carved and inlaid wooden boxes, chests and furniture. Haggling is the norm.

Key
- ▲ Church
- 🔺 Hindu Temple
- ⊕ Hospital
- Ⓗ Hotel
- ✉ Main Post Office
- Station
- 𝑖 Tourist information
- *Jumma Masjid* Places of interest

4
a Use information in **Source F** to draw a graph showing population change in Mumbai.
b Describe the pattern shown by the graph.
c London's population is estimated to reach 6.1 million in 2001. How does Mumbai's population compare with London's?

5 Use **Source G** to describe the location of Mumbai.

6 Use evidence from **Source H** to support or reject the following statements. Give reasons for your views.
- Mumbai has had some British influence.
- Mumbai is an important port.
- Mumbai would make an interesting holiday destination.
- Mumbai is very much like a city in an MEDC.

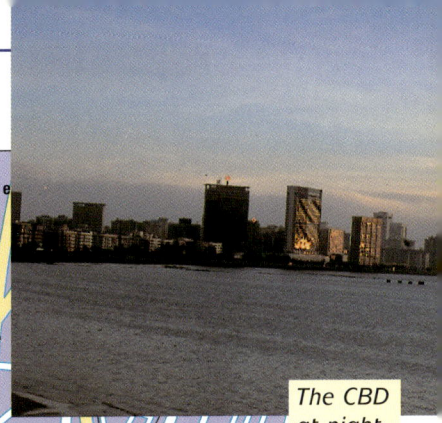

How do housing opportunities vary in Mumbai?

What factors determine people's access to housing and services in Mumbai?

1.10 A kind of living?

The Mumbai that tourists don't see

Mumbai's population rise is the result of two separate processes: inward **migration** from the surrounding rural areas and a natural increase in population. While families in urban areas of India tend to have smaller families than those in rural areas, better levels of healthcare keep many people alive longer.

On balance, the result is population increase. Mumbai has a growth rate of 4% each year. Such growth makes it extremely difficult for the Mumbai authorities to provide the basic services. There is also an inability to provide acceptable levels of housing for all. Variations in housing quality are great. There are some areas of Mumbai that the authorities would prefer tourists not to see or know about!

A Contrasts in shelter, Mumbai

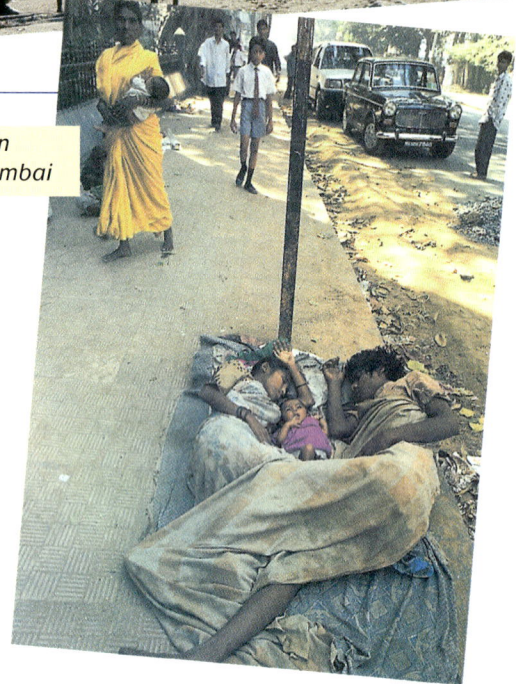

B The location of slum community Sanjay Gandhi Nagar – past and present

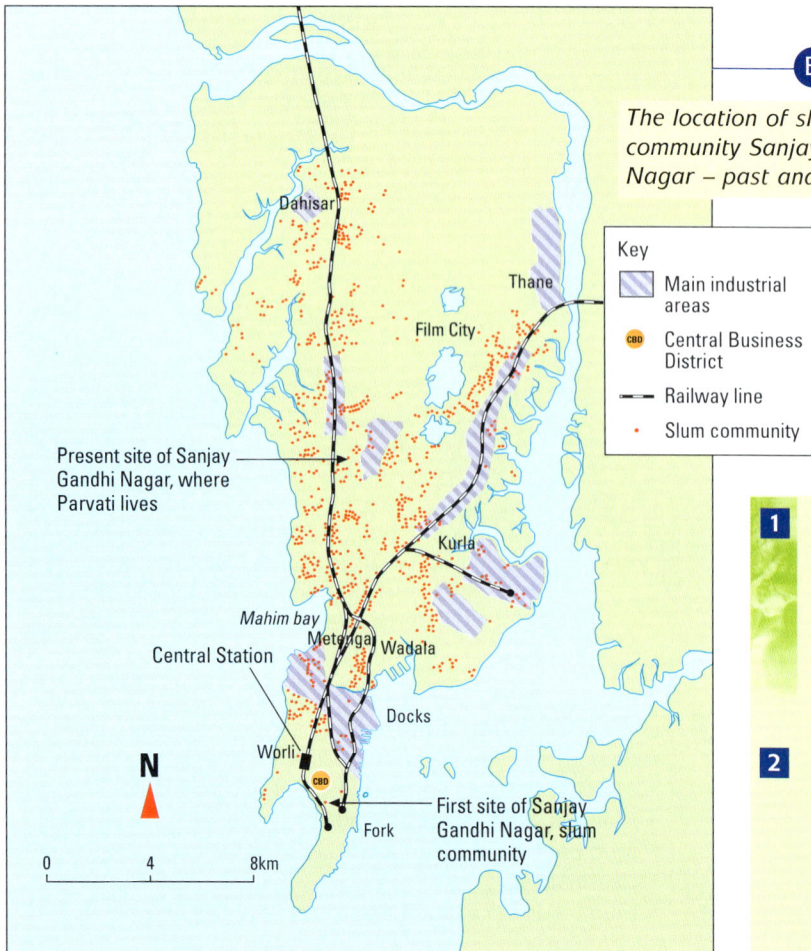

Key

- Main industrial areas
- **CBD** Central Business District
- ▬ Railway line
- • Slum community

Present site of Sanjay Gandhi Nagar, where Parvati lives

Dahisar

Thane

Film City

Kurla

Mahim bay

Metenga Wadala

Central Station

Docks

Worli

CBD

Fork

First site of Sanjay Gandhi Nagar, slum community

N

0   4   8km

1 Look at **Source A**.
  a Describe each of the three types of shelter shown in the two photographs.
  b Rank them according to the opportunities they appear to give for a high quality of life.
  c Compare your rank order with those of other members of your group.

2 Look at **Source B**.
  a Describe the relationship between slums and
     (i) the railway lines
     (ii) the main industrial areas.
  b Suggest reasons for the relationships you have described.

Moving a slum community

1976 A construction company leased a piece of wasteland to house its workers.

1979 When the lease ran out the workers stayed. Other people joined them. The slum covered one hectare in an area of otherwise smart high-rise buildings.

1980 Sanjay Gandhi Nagar demolished by Municipal Authorities in 1980, 1981 and 1982. The people rebuilt their houses. In 1982 Nivara Hakk, a **Non-Governmental organization (NGO)** stepped in. The slum could stay if the residents agreed to be moved to the suburbs in the future.

1982 A Residents' Association was registered and a school established. 10 rupees (about 20 pence) a month was taken from residents towards the cost of a future move.

1985 Slum dwellers informed that their huts were liable to be demolished. The same night a fire swept through the slum destroying it and killing a child. The State Government announced aid of 100 rupees per person. The people rebuilt.

1986 12 March. Slum destroyed again. Police and municipal workers invaded the site and evicted the dwellers. Construction materials taken away in trucks. The slum dwellers tried to re-occupy the land. They were accompanied by influential members of Nivara Hakk including a journalist, a human rights lawyer, a film producer and Shabana Azmi, an actress.

Truncheon-wielding police herded them into vans.

The next day the news hit the papers, mainly because of the celebrities involved.

The people remained on the pavement in the area.

1 May. A twelve-year-old boy was knocked down and killed by a car. Slum dwellers occupied the office of a local official in protest and two residents and Shabana Azmi began a hunger strike to demand alternative accommodation.

The residents of Sanjay Gandhi Nagar were given new land in the suburbs.

Source: Adapted from 'The fire, a death and the cooking pots', by Jeremy Seabrook, New Internationalist, May 1997

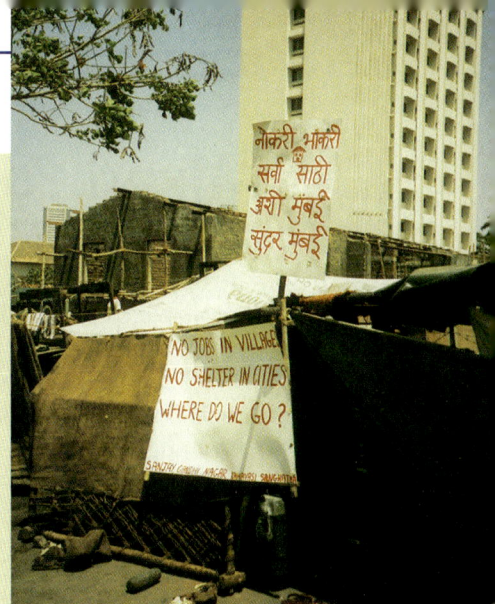

E

C

'The slums are a danger. The boys and men are beggars and thieves who need to be closely policed. The women bathe in public and have no thought to modesty.'

'City slums are full of hard working people who help each other and are capable of enduring great hardships. Many perform underpaid tasks for the rich of the city and would not have the living conditions they do if they were properly paid.'

D *Different views*

A journey to work

'Parvati works two hours a day in each of four houses, and earns 200 rupees a month at each house. The train fare costs 100 rupees a month and the bus half as much again. All of this has been added to her costs since she and the rest of Sanjay Gandhi Nagar were evicted from this area ten years ago. An hour and a half each way, sometimes two hours – time erased from her life. Over a period of ten years, that represents several months in a train or bus, day or night.'

Source: 'The city, our stepmother' by Jeremy Seabrook, New Internationalist, May 1997

3 Look at **Source C**.
   a Describe the roles played by slum dwellers, the NGO and the authorities in the events at Sanjay Gandhi Nagar between 1980 and 1986.
   b Discuss which groups had the greatest and the least power.
   c How does the photograph help explain the problems faced by the slum dwellers?

4 Look at **Source D**.
   a Explain why some people wished to remove residents from Sanjay Gandhi Nagar.
   b With which view do you most agree? Explain your choice.
   c How might you have acted as a local government official at Sanjay Gandhi Nagar in 1986? Explain your actions.

5 Study **Sources E** and **B**.
   a Describe the location of the present Sanjay Gandhi Nagar.
   b How does this compare with its first site?
   b Describe the daily journey made by Parvati.
   c Suggest how the move to the present site has affected her quality of life.

1.11 Mixed fortunes

How does people's access to housing and services change with time?
In what ways are individuals and organizations able to influence housing decisions?

The people of Sanjay Gandhi Nagar were located onto a new site in 1987. It is more than 20 kilometres north of the old site. The land was owned by the Dinshaw Trust, a local charity. The Trust gave each family a plot of land measuring five metres by four metres. On this they built their houses. In the first ten years since the move only about 60 new families had moved in. This was the result of a decision by the Residents' Association. It decided that individuals could only sell their houses back to the Association. In this way it could stop huge profits being made by selling them to outsiders. The Association can also approve future buyers. The new community has a settled and safe feel which is unusual for slum dwellings.

- Permanent shops and restaurants
- The little streets are neat and most houses are very clean.
- The quarry used for housing stone is now half-filled with waste covered in bright green algae
- Garbage dumps attract flies and mosquitoes. The council use a liquid pesticide
- Public toilets are close to the houses
- Houses are well spaced and housing density, at 300 families to a hectare, is low for slum communities
- There is an area of open space in the centre
- The electricity supply, paid for by the Residents' Association, is unreliable
- Water taps only operate between 2:00 a.m. and 5:00 a.m. Women fill any containers they can for that day's supply

Features of the new Sanjay Gandhi Nagar

A plan for the present site of Sanjay Gandhi Nagar

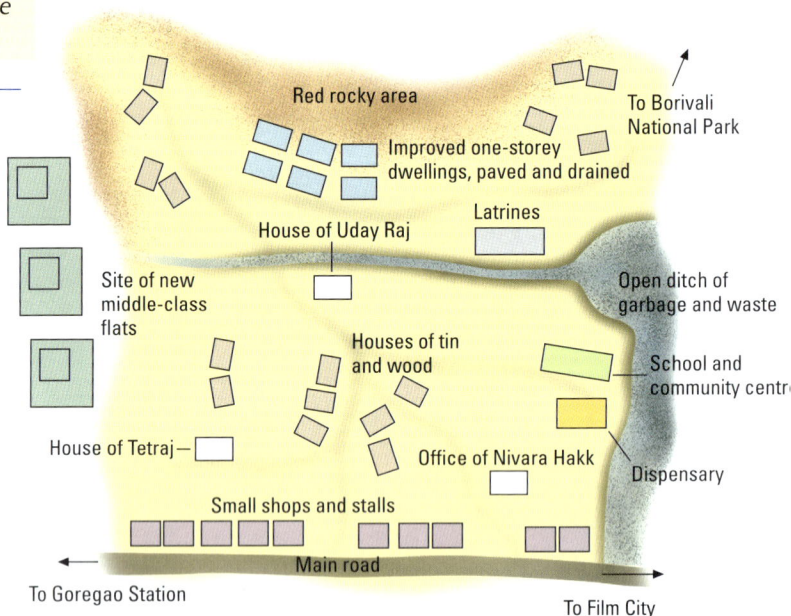

A

B *A divide has formed between those who have become richer and those who have stayed poorer*

Tetraj lives in a house improved by a grant of $250 from CASPLAN, a German NGO. It has a tiled floor, a big wooden bed and an electric fan. There is a tin chair for visitors. Her husband sells puri (a spicy chickpea dish) from a cart and earns about 100 rupees a day.

B R Salve had his arm amputated as a child. He has worked for the city for 19 years. His wife earns 200 rupees a month at three different houses*. Their house is poor. Metal walls are corroded. Food is prepared on a small concrete platform and a low concrete wall separates a bathing area from their living space. Clothes hang from nails on a wall and there is a black and white television.

Uday Raj has moved on from being a taxi driver when he earned 3 000 rupees a month to owning a number of taxis which he rents to other drivers. He has loaned money to other members of the community which makes them dependent on him. His house reflects his status and wealth. Uday has ambitions to become a member of the Maharashtra State Legislative Assembly.

* At the time of writing, there were roughly 67 rupees to the pound

1 Look at **Source A**.
a Describe the boundaries of Sanjay Gandhi Nagar.
b List those features of the settlement which are likely to:
(i) improve quality of life
(ii) reduce quality of life.
Explain your choices in each case.
c Give reasons for the locations of the shops and stalls.
d Suggest how the new middle-class flats may affect the lives of residents of Sanjay Gandhi Nagar.

2 Look at **Source B**.
a Rank the three residents according to wealth.
b How does this affect their housing conditions?
c What else affects their living conditions?
d Suggest how differences in wealth may work against a community spirit.

New Slum Redevelopment Scheme

The Government of Maharashtra State has come up with an idea for rehousing slum dwellers – and it won't cost them a rupee! The scheme will allow all who arrived in Mumbai before 1 January 1995 to be given a free house. The land on which the slums now stand will be sold to construction companies providing they build concrete apartments for all of the slum dwellers.
Each household will get a 70 square metre apartment in a multi-storey building on the same site and the developer will be permitted to build houses for sale on the remaining land.

C

D *Hopes for the future*

Tetraj said, 'If we are offered an apartment we will sell it and return to the countryside of Uttar Pradesh where we will buy a plot of land'. Tetraj does not know that in her home district land prices have been rising rapidly and she would only be able to afford a small plot with the money she would be likely to make from the sale of an apartment. This would be barely enough to feed the family.

Uday Raj feels that the scheme offers riches to everyone. He believes firmly in the promises of the **Shiv Sena/BJP** and in their statement that people will be housed in transitional dwellings between the knocking down of the slums and the building of the apartments.

'This is something which the people's movements and NGOs must use to our advantage. We cannot necessarily take it at face value. If it is something more than an election gimmick, it must be part of a longer term strategy to get the poor to leave Mumbai. But that isn't going to stop others coming [from rural areas]. In fact, even if people go home [to their village] with what seems a small fortune, it will soon be used up on buying a piece of land, building a house, or just surviving. Either they or their children will be forced to migrate to Mumbai all over again, once again with nothing, to squat in new, insecure slums on the far periphery of the city.'

E *Gurbir Singh of the NGO Nivara Hakk states...*

F *Percentages of urban and rural people living in poverty in selected LEDCs*

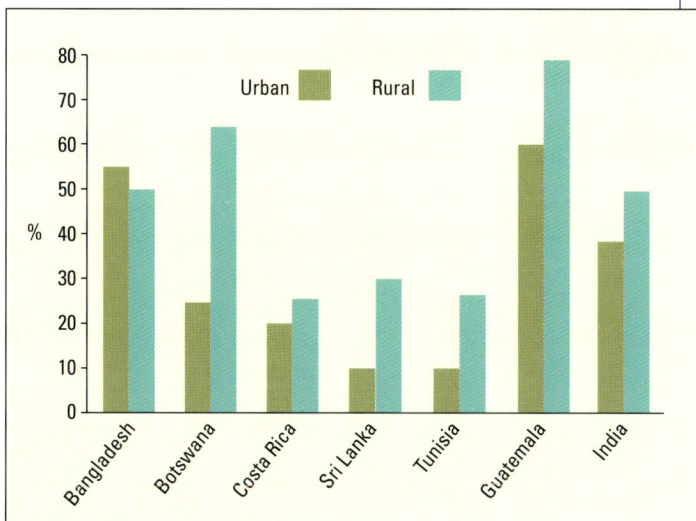

3 Look at **Source C**.
a Describe the scheme.
b Outline the advantages of the scheme to:
(i) the slum dwellers
(ii) the State Government.

4 Look at **Source D**.
a Describe the feelings of the two residents of Sanjay Gandhi Nagar.
b Why is Tetraj likely to be disappointed?
c What could happen to upset Uday Raj's view of the scheme?

5 Study **Source E**.
a What is Nivara Hakk?
b What are its views on the proposal?
c Suggest why it holds these views?

6 a Describe what the graph in **Source F** shows about poverty in India.
b How does this evidence support the views of Nivara Hakk?

7 Would you improve living conditions for slum dwellers or encourage them to migrate back to the villages? Explain your view.

27

1.12 Two cities compared

Leicester – a city in an MEDC

Although all cities are unique, those within a particular country often have a similar history. This often allows them to develop similar patterns. Patterns in different parts of the world may be compared. In MEDCs the patterns can be very different to cities in LEDCs. This is especially true for patterns of housing.

B *Pre-1918 terraced housing*

C *Post-1945 private housing*

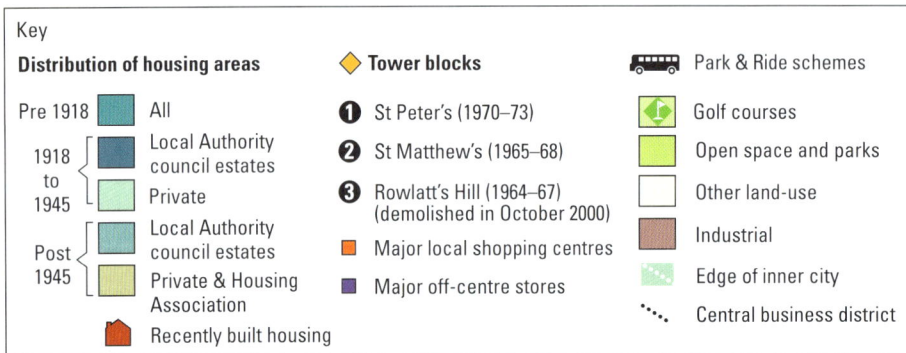

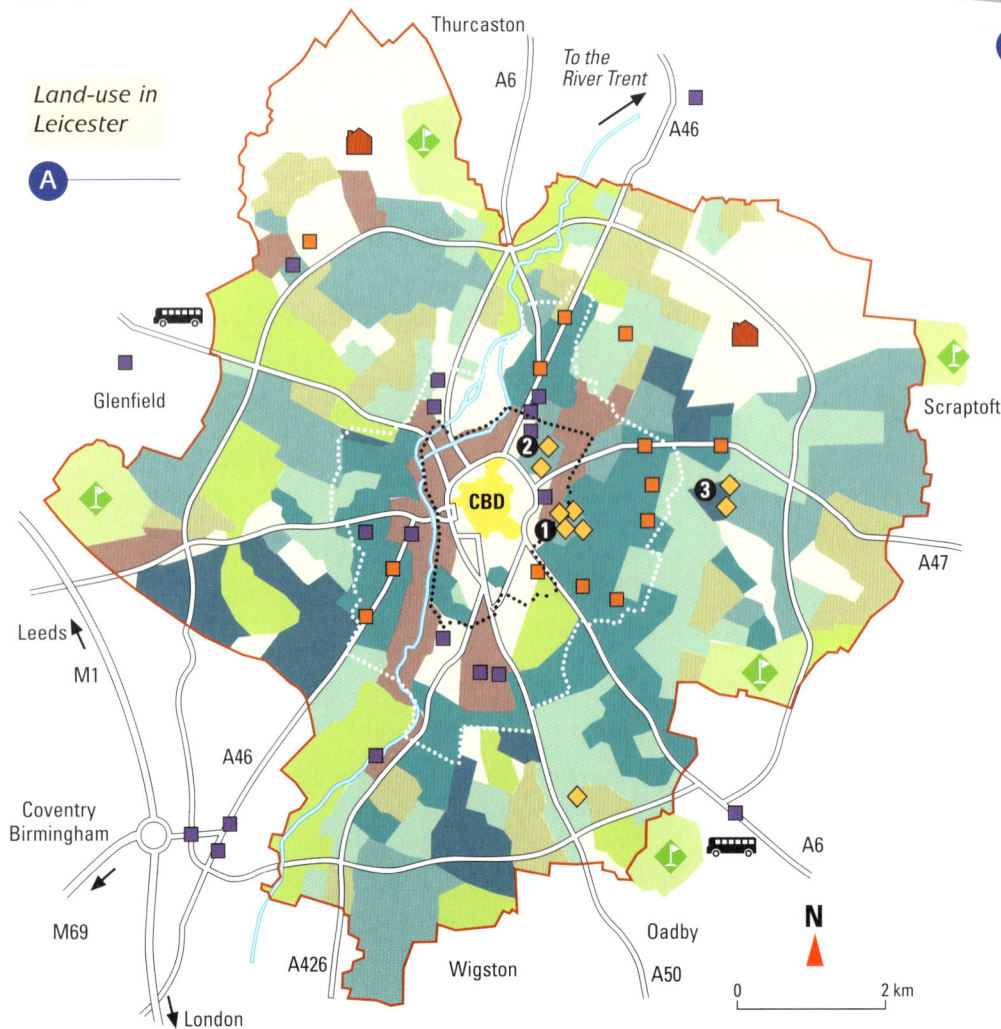

Key

Distribution of housing areas

Pre 1918 — All

1918 to 1945 — Local Authority council estates / Private

Post 1945 — Local Authority council estates / Private & Housing Association

Recently built housing

◆ **Tower blocks**
❶ St Peter's (1970–73)
❷ St Matthew's (1965–68)
❸ Rowlatt's Hill (1964–67) (demolished in October 2000)
■ Major local shopping centres
■ Major off-centre stores

Park & Ride schemes
Golf courses
Open space and parks
Other land-use
Industrial
Edge of inner city
Central business district

Land-use in Leicester

A

Thurcaston, A6, To the River Trent, A46, Glenfield, Scraptoft, CBD, A47, Leeds, M1, A46, Coventry Birmingham, M69, A426, Wigston, Oadby, A50, A6, London

N   0   2 km

1
a Use **Source A** to describe the distribution of pre-1918 housing in Leicester.
b Compare this with the distribution of post-1945 housing and recently built housing areas.

2 Look at **Sources B** and **C**.
a List differences between the two housing types.
b Suggest how the amenities in each of these housing types may:
 • have changed with time
 • be similar and different today

3
a Describe the availability and distribution of **one type** of service from the map. Choose from:
 • shopping services
 • open space and parks
 • golf courses
 • the park-and-ride scheme
b Suggest reasons for the distribution of your chosen service.

28

Mexico City – a city in an LEDC

While the population of the city of Leicester is falling due to counter-urbanization, Mexico City, the capital of Mexico, continues to grow. The most recent census showed that over 17 million people live here, but the number is now much greater than this as migrants arrive every day from the countryside and birth rates remain high. The local government cannot provide housing and services for so many people. The pattern of housing in Mexico City is similar to many LEDC cities but different from most MEDC cities.

D Land-use in Mexico City

Key

Housing areas

- Rich
- Medium
- Poor
- Other land use
- Commercial and industrial areas
- Main roads

City Centre

N

0 2 4 6 8 10 km

E Rich housing in Mexico City

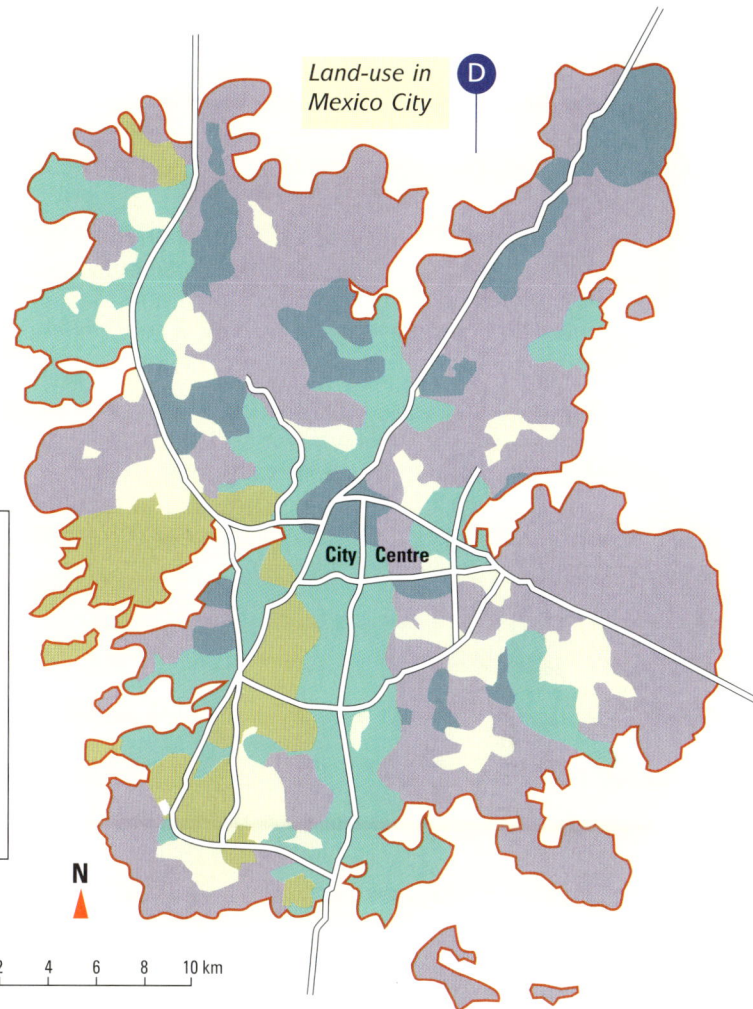

F Poor housing (a barrio) in Mexico City

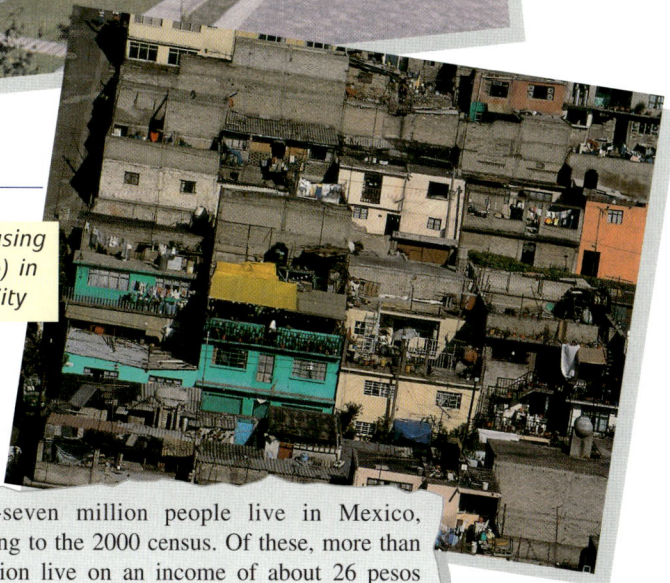

Ninety-seven million people live in Mexico, according to the 2000 census. Of these, more than 40 million live on an income of about 26 pesos (about £2) or less per day. Fourteen million live in houses with dirt floors and more than six million live in shacks with cardboard roofs. Many of these live in Mexico City. Health care is improving. Infant mortality rates have dropped by half and children under five are less likely to die. Basic health care now reaches 99.5% of Mexicans and children attend school for an average of 7.6 years.

G Slow but steady progress?

Adapted from the *Financial Times*, 14 December 2000

---

4 Look at **Source D**.
   a Use an atlas to describe the location of Mexico City.
   b What is the west-east distance across Mexico City at its widest point?
   c How does this compare with Leicester?

5 a Describe the distribution of 'poor' housing in Mexico City?
   b Compare this with the distribution of the pre-1918 housing in Leicester.

6 a Compare the housing shown in **Sources E** and **F** in terms of
      • type • site • possible amenities.
   b In which of the two cities does the contrast in housing appear the greater? Explain your answer.

7 Read **Source G**.
   a Suggest how life in Mexico City is different when compared to life in a city in an MEDC like Leicester. Refer to:
      • housing conditions
      • infant mortality rates
      • average years spent at school
      • income and spending power.
   b Suggest ways in which the authorities could improve the quality of life in Mexico City.

1 Communities can change services

Investigating change

The Spinney Hill area of Leicester is an inner city terraced area into which a large Asian community has moved since the 1960s. Emma and Majid were interested in investigating how local services had changed to meet the community needs.

On their first visit, Majid checked the use of buildings against their use shown in a 1970 Directory (**Source B**) while Emma did a field study of current building use (**Source C**). They were surprised to record that the buildings had hardly changed but the services in them were now very different.

Al Shafqat Travel and Bolton Halal Poultry have replaced 241 Mere Road and Fiveways Furniture at 89 St Peter's Road

The old Evington cinema is now used as Sheltered Housing for the Asian community and is managed by Fara estates

A

B Spinney Hill building use 1970

St Peter's Road

(odd)
83 Farouq – butcher
85 Private house
87 Private house
89 Fiveways Furniture

(even)
88 Private house
90 Runswick – hairdressers
92 Hallam – fruit shop

Laurel Road
2 Private house

Eggington Street

(odd)
1 Jarvis – betting shop
3 Savage – chemist
5 Tailby – newsagent
7 Reesby – draper

(even)
2 Harwar – butcher
4 and 6 Sturdon – grocer

East Park Road
378 Evington Cinema

Mere Road
241 Private house
243 Private house

Key

▨ (yellow)	Food shops
▨ (blue)	Goods and services
▨ (brown)	Community services
▢	Terraced houses
⋈	Traffic calming

C Use of buildings 2001

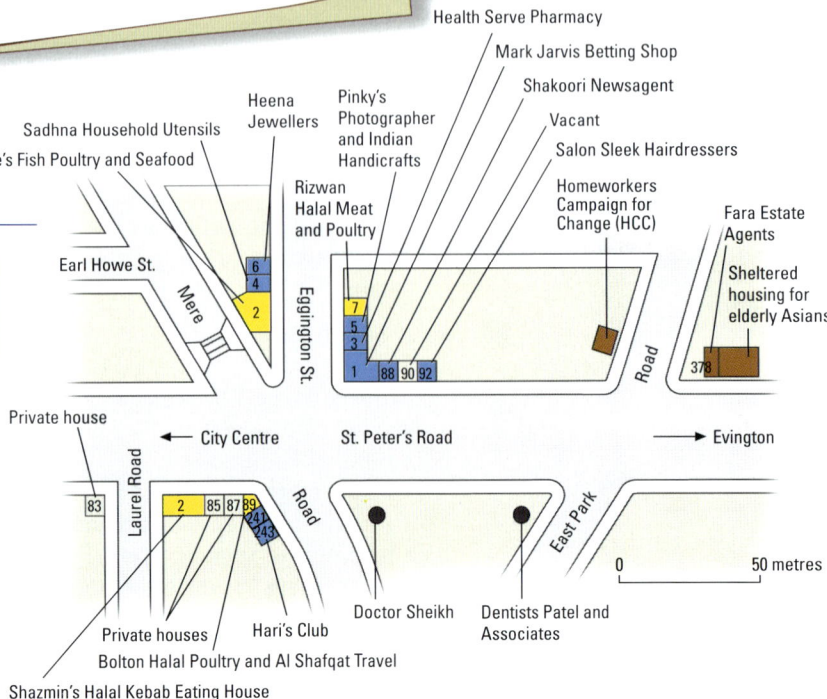

Sadhna Household Utensils
Heena Jewellers
Pinky's Photographer and Indian Handicrafts
Health Serve Pharmacy
Mark Jarvis Betting Shop
Shakoori Newsagent
Vacant
Salon Sleek Hairdressers
Howe's Fish Poultry and Seafood
Rizwan Halal Meat and Poultry
Homeworkers Campaign for Change (HCC)
Fara Estate Agents
Sheltered housing for elderly Asians
Earl Howe St.
Mere
Eggington St.
Road
Private house
← City Centre
St. Peter's Road
Evington →
Laurel Road
Road
East Park
Private house
Private houses
Hari's Club
Bolton Halal Poultry and Al Shafqat Travel
Shazmin's Halal Kebab Eating House
Doctor Sheikh
Dentists Patel and Associates
0   50 metres

1 Study **Sources A** and **B**.
a What are the current uses of 89 St Peter's Road and 241 Mere Road?
b What was the Fara Estates building used for in 1970?

2 Study **Sources B** and **C**.
a Draw up a table comparing the use of buildings in 1970 and today.
b What type of services are present today? Suggest why the local community wanted these services close by.
c Have any 1970 building uses survived? Suggest why.
d Explain how the local community benefits from these changes.

3 Carry out a similar field survey of an area where a changing community has caused a change in services.

2

Changing the urban environment

KEY IDEAS

Changes in housing and service provision affect the pattern of inequality in urban areas.

Conflicts often occur between different groups of people when changes are planned and/or implemented in urban areas. Some groups of people have more power to bring about or resist these changes than others.

CARDIFF BAY
Music Festival

The regeneration of Cardiff Bay has enabled many new developments to be built on the waterfront, but these changes to the urban environment have not been without some conflicts

2.1 Change in Cardiff Bay

Nineteenth-century growth

Many cities in MEDCs grew as a result of the Industrial Revolution. In many places this was because there was coal and iron ore close by. Being a port gave Cardiff an extra advantage. Other materials could be imported and iron and steel products exported. In the nineteenth century these cities prospered and unemployment was rare.

Until the end of the eighteenth century much of the medieval parish of St Mary was salt marsh and rough grazing known as The Moors.

In 1774 the Ironmasters of Merthyr Tydfil built the Glamorganshire Canal to transport iron from their works to Cardiff.

The second Marquis of Bute planned the development of the area in the early 1800s. His development included a new main road – Bute Street, a railway from Merthyr Tydfil to Cardiff and the Bute Dock.

B *The working docks*

By 1907 there were 67 hectares (165 acres) of docks and in 1913 over 13.5 million tonnes of exports, which included almost 10.5 million tonnes of coal.

A *Cardiff – an excellent industrial location*

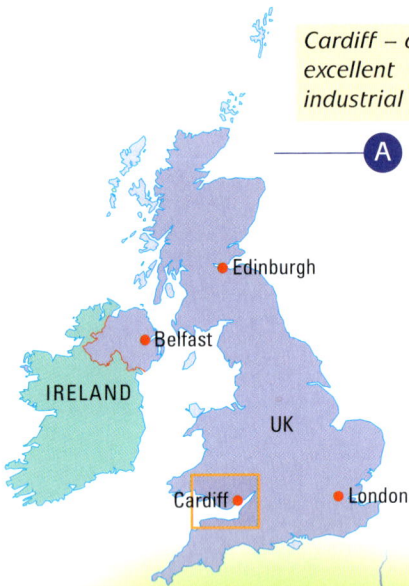

Key

▨	South Wales coalfield. Source of coal and iron ore
■	Site of ironworks
◆	Site of steelworks
■	Imports
■	Exports
∼	Rivers

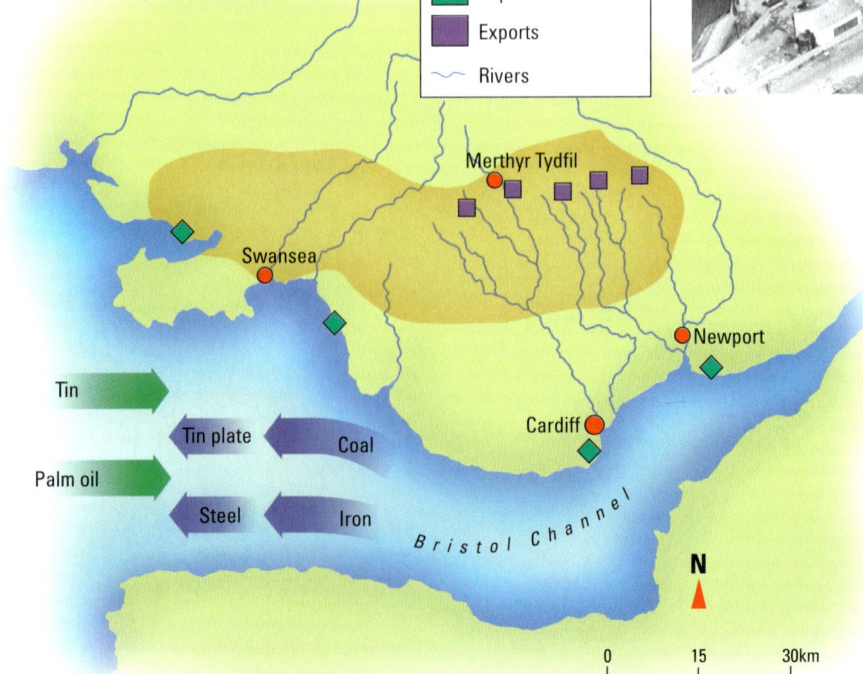

1
  a Use **Source A** and an atlas to describe the location of Cardiff.
  b Explain how and why Cardiff's location helped the city to become important in the Industrial Revolution.

2
  a Draw an outline sketch of **Source B** and label the following land uses:
   • docks   • roads
   • railways   • water.
   • warehouses
  b List the statements from **Source B** in their correct time order.
  c Imagine you took this aerial photo from a plane. Radio back your report on the scene below.

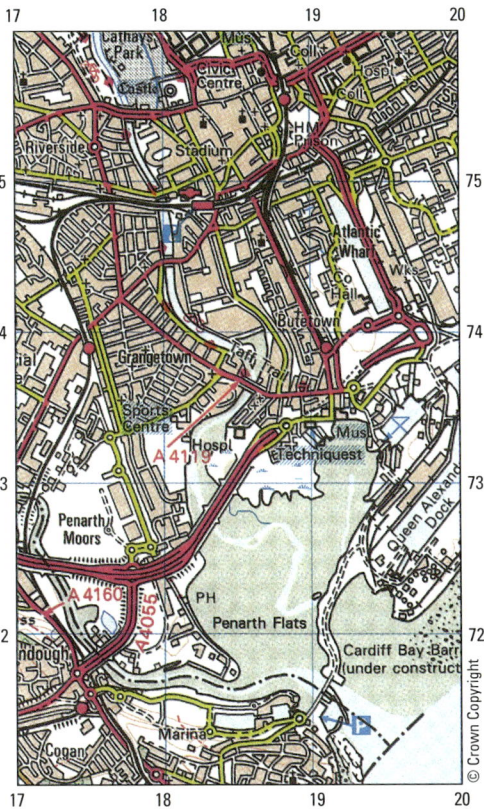

C OS (1: 50 000 scale) map extract of the Cardiff Bay area

D Cardiff Bay Barrage

The £197 million Barrage was essential to the development because Cardiff has a tidal range of fourteen metres, one of the largest in the world. At low tide the Bay is inaccessible for up to fourteen hours a day. With the Barrage, the waterfront environment becomes a permanent feature and this will attract new housing and service developments. In use since November 1999, the Barrage holds back the rivers Taff and Ely to create a large freshwater bay of 200 hectares whose waves lap onto 5km of prime waterfront. It has however permanently flooded tidal saltwater mudflats – an area of international scientific interest for birds.

Adapted from *Cardiff Bay Development Newsletters*

E

Twentieth-century decline and change

After reaching a peak of exports in 1913, Cardiff docks began to handle fewer materials and products. There were several reasons for this:

- overseas markets were lost during and after the First World War (1914-1918)
- other countries began to produce their own iron and steel so reducing demand
- local coal and iron ore began to run out and became expensive to mine.

This decline continued until, by the mid-1980s, there was high unemployment and out-migration leaving a huge area of derelict wasteland with empty houses and warehouses by the waterfront. To tackle these problems and regenerate the city, the *Cardiff Bay Development Corporation* (CBDC) was created in 1987. The single most important part of the development was the creation of the Cardiff Bay Barrage.

3 a Why did Cardiff docks go into decline after 1913?
b Discuss the effects of this decline on different groups of people.

4 Study **Sources C** and **D**.
a Give six-figure grid references for each end of the barrage.
b Estimate in km^2 the area of mudflats that will be covered by the freshwater bay.
c In which direction was the camera pointing to take **Source D**?
d List the grid squares that contain the area in the photo.

5 Study **Sources D** and **E**.
a What is the purpose of the barrage?
b Why was it essential to build the barrage before housing and service improvements could take place on the waterfront?
c What is your view on the impact of the barrage on the environment?

6 Read your radio report in your answer to question 2c. Use **Sources B** and **D** to discuss how different this report would be if you flew over Cardiff Bay today.

2.2 Changing Cardiff for the better?

A Cardiff – getting there

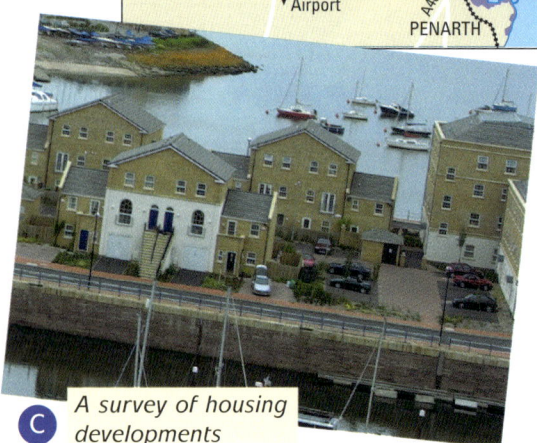

Eventually 6000 new apartments and houses will be built in Cardiff Bay. Of these, 1500 must be **social housing** to meet the needs of local people including low-cost affordable housing. This should ensure a good mix of houses accessible to all pockets. There will be a range of housing from five-bedroom detached houses, costing up to £550 000, to small apartments, starting at about £70 000. At Pengam Green, a mixture of private houses and low-cost community housing is being completed.

Source: Adapted from various *Cardiff Bay factsheets*

B The CBDC's housing strategy

C A survey of housing developments

The Mermaid Quay Experience provides a shopping and leisure complex on the waterfront

As part of her study into the changing urban environment, a student contacted house-builders to find out about housing being built in the Bay. The results are shown in the table below.

Company	Price range	Type	Location
Beazer Homes	From £86 950	Apartments (1/2/3 bed)	The Plaza
Bellway Homes	£79 995 – £110 500	Apartments/townhouses	Atlantic Wharf
Bellway Homes	£105 000 – £170,000	Apartments/townhouses	Marquis Court
Persimmon	£70 000 – £117 250	Detached houses (3/4 bed)	Pengam Green
Redrow	From £95 000	Apartments (1/2 bed)	Schooner Way
St David's	£70 000 – £550 000	Apartments/townhouses	Adventurer's Quay
Wimpey	From £95 950	Apartments (2 bed)	The Plaza

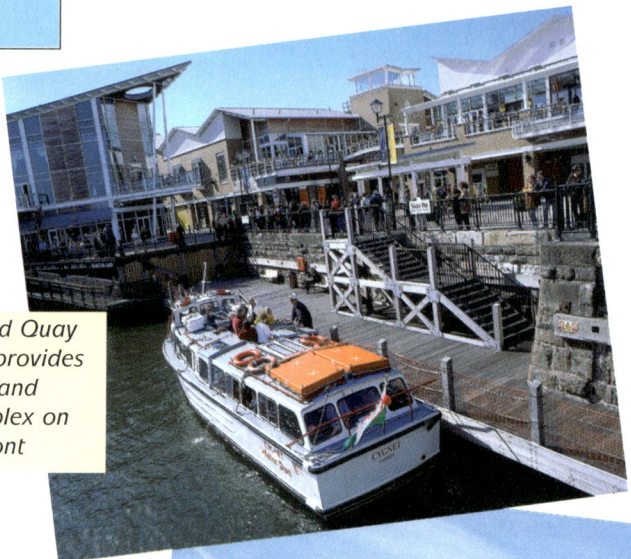

Housing alone is not enough!

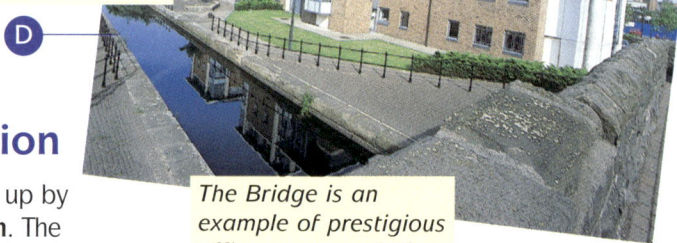

D

The Bridge is an example of prestigious office accommodation

The Cardiff Bay Development Corporation

The *Cardiff Bay Development Corporation* (CBDC) was one of twelve set up by the UK government in 1987 to tackle the problems of **urban dereliction**. The CBDC had no planning powers of its own so it has had to work closely with:
• local councils in the Cardiff area
• private owners (such as Associated British Ports).

Together they set out to meet the needs of local people while also attracting inward investment and new residents to regenerate the bay area of the city.

The CBDC's work was completed in March 2000. Future developments are being managed by the *Cardiff Harbour Authority*. In its thirteen years the CBDC went a long way towards making Cardiff a desirable city in which to live and work. This has been achieved by changing the urban environment.

1 The map in **Source A** was produced for a brochure about new housing in Cardiff. Suggest why it shows the following:
• the M4 and its junctions
• directions to London, Swansea and the airport
• the A roads leading to the Bay area.

Map of Cardiff Bay area showing labelled locations:

- To the Millennium Stadium
- Cardiff Bay Arts Trust Information Centre
- Exchange Building
- Baltic House
- The Point
- Butetown History & Arts Centre
- Craft in the Bay
- Atlantic Wharf UCI Cinema Hollywood Bowl Restaurants & Nightclubs
- Proposed Wales Millennium Centre site
- Scott Harbour
- Adventurers' Quay Housing
- Crickhowell House
- National Assembly of Wales
- Roath Basin
- Public Piazza
- Mermaid Quay Retail/Leisure
- Techniquest
- NCM
- Lightship 2000
- Pierhead Building
- Millennium Waterfront
- Visitor Centre
- Norwegian Church Arts Centre
- St David's hotel & spa

Street labels: Bute Street, Collingdon Road, West Bute Street, James Street, Bute Crescent, Bute Place, Adelaide Street, Stuart Street, Pierhead Street, Britannia Quay, Harbour Drive, A4232

Key

P	Car parks
(orange)	Buildings of interest
(green)	Parks
(olive)	Other buildings
(blue)	Banks
(brown)	Pubs/restaurants
WC	Toilets
B	Bus stop
☆	Public art

Scale: 0 – 100m, N (north arrow)

E *Providing new services*

2 Study page 31 and **Sources B** and **C**.
  a How did the CBDC try to ensure that housing was accessible to different income groups and local people?
  b Why do you think this aim was part of its housing strategy?
  c Which groups of people do you think the house prices are targeted to attract – local people or people from places outside Cardiff? Justify your view.

3 Study **Source D**. Suggest groups of people who would benefit from the other developments shown. Explain why.

4 Use **Source E** and other information to plan a two-hour tour of the Cardiff Bay area for yourself and your family. Explain your choice of places to visit.

5 Read **Source F**.
  a Explain how the Community Initiatives Programme works.
  b Why is it important to develop community activities when changing an urban environment?
  c Prepare a bid to the CIP for an event you wish to organise in the Cardiff Bay area.

6 The mission of the CBDC in 1987 was 'To put Cardiff on the international map as a superlative maritime city'. To what extent do you think this has been achieved? Refer to advantages and disadvantages to different groups of people in your evaluation.

F *The Community Initiatives Programme (CIP)*

'The CBDC provided money for the CIP to give grants to develop events and activities. Most grants support links with schools, youth clubs, voluntary and community groups. We encourage them to develop activities that help regenerate a new community within Cardiff. It is important to remember that any development is not just about the housing and other services – the people who are going to live here and use them must also be provided for. We are especially concerned with education and training for employment, combating disadvantage, improving community relations and encouraging safety for children.'

2.3 Safety in cities

'Well I don't like the feeling that I've got to take the car everywhere. I would like to be as free as I was years back... you could leave your door open years ago, now the first thing you do when you come in the door is shut it, lock it and bolt it. You know, so it's different. You feel as if sometimes you're in a fort. You know, for security, to protect yourself against other human beings. It infuriates me, sometimes, thinking, "hell, I would like a nice walk" or something like that.'

Diana, Edinburgh

Source: "Social Geographies of Women's Fear of Crime"

A Some public places and certain times are perceived as more dangerous than others

Bright lights – safe city?

All towns and cities have places where people feel unsafe to go. These have often developed a poor image from the past which is difficult to shake off even though they may have become safer. People do not want to live in these no-go areas and avoid using their services.

Most cities, though, are much safer now than they were in the nineteenth century. Disease, crime, and poor housing were common then and policing was not as effective as it is today. Many councils are using funds to make cities even safer to live and work in.

BRITISH TOURISTS MUGGED IN FLORIDA

Central Park only safe during day, says New York Times

Backpacker kidnapped in centre of Sydney

RIOTS AND FIGHTING CONTINUE IN JERUSALEM – TOURISTS ADVISED TO STAY AWAY

B Safety is an issue around the world

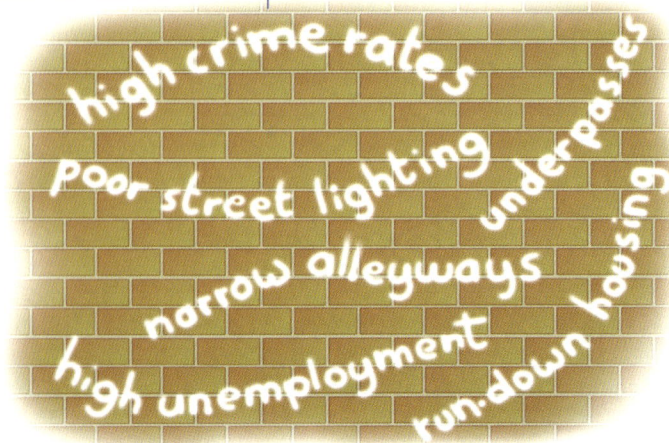

C Six common features of unsafe urban areas

high crime rates

poor street lighting

narrow alleyways

underpasses

high unemployment

run-down housing

1 Read what Diana says in **Source A**.
   a What differences does she describe between life in the past and her life now?
   b Describe her feelings.

2 Study **Source B**.
   a What safety issues are mentioned in each named place?
   b Add some examples of your own.

3 Study **Source C**.
   a List the **six** features of unsafe urban areas.
   b Add **two** other features to your list.
   c Rank your list from 1–8 according to how easy you think it is to reduce the problem. Justify your order.

The Urban Regeneration Committee of Lincoln City Council installed a CCTV system in the city centre

Lincoln City Football in the Community Scheme

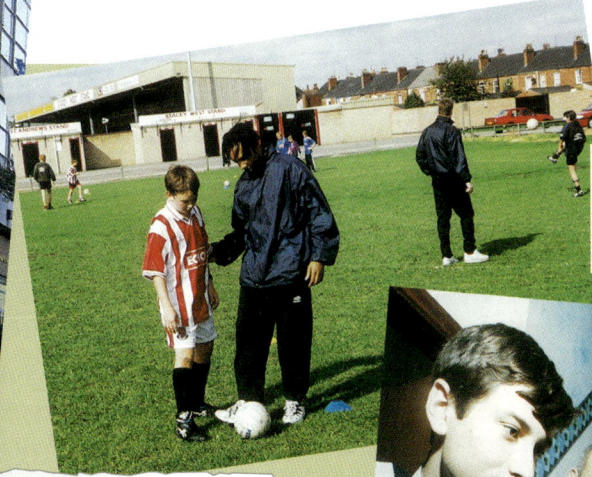

Personal attack alarms were given out to women, the elderly and previous victims of crime

Educational package on crime and drug abuse delivered to children through theatre group Cragrats

Regular issues of The Community Partner, the Lincolnshire Safer Cities Project newsletter, were circulated to public places in the city

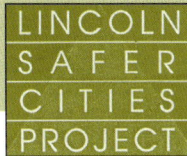

LINCOLN SAFER CITIES PROJECT

The Lincoln Safer Cities Project ran from 1995 until 1998

Lincolnshire Police Volunteer Cadets installed door chains and viewers

Safer City Project strategies in Lincoln

D

The Safer Cities Project ... and an Urban Challenge!

Various governments have provided money to city councils to make urban areas even safer and more accessible. Between 1988 and 1998, the Safer Cities Project provided money to tackle problems of above-average crime rates and the fear of crime in inner city areas. Since 1998 this has been replaced by money from the Urban Challenge Fund.

Both projects involve the local community in identifying safety issues and sharing solutions with decision-makers to make cities safer and more accessible to different groups of people at any time of the day or night.

In 1998 Urban Challenge money was used to continue the work of Lincoln's Safe City Project. It produced the Lincoln City Crime and Disorder Reduction Strategy 1999-2002. This has seven main objectives.

4
a What was the Safer Cities Project?
b Suggest why it involved a partnership between local government and communities.

5 Look at **Source D**.
a Describe those features of Lincoln's Safer Cities Project that were intended to tackle:
   (i) the causes of crime
   (ii) the fear of crime.
b Explain how different groups of people will have benefited from these strategies in Lincoln.

6 Look at **Source E**.
a Surrounding the table of Urban Challenge objectives are seven examples of methods being used in Lincoln. Draw a two-column table and match these up to each objective.
b Choose **one** objective that interests you and devise an illustrated poster to advertise how you would tackle the issue.

CCTV schemes in the estates

Involve the community in partnerships

Extend Pub Watch schemes

Reduce unemployment by increasing training

challenge URBAN

Urban Challenge objectives
1 To reduce crime and disorder in Abbey Ward, Park Ward, the city centre, the St Giles and Birchwood estates
2 To reduce crimes of violence, burglary in the home, domestic violence and auto crime
3 To reduce the fear of crime amongst women and the elderly
4 To reduce substance misuse
5 To divert young people from committing crime and becoming the victims of crime
6 To encourage, develop and facilitate the partnership approach to crime reduction
7 To identify and develop projects to tackle the underlying causes of crime

Target drugs suppliers

Develop detached youth work

Use the media to present a balanced picture of crime against the elderly

E *Urban Challenge Priorities in Lincoln*

2.4 A question of attitude

Over one in ten people in MEDCs are classed as being permanently disabled. This figure is almost certain to increase as people live longer. Added to this are those people who are temporarily disabled, for example, those with broken limbs.

It has been argued that people are not disadvantaged by their disabilities but by the way in which society treats them. Most cities have not been planned to enable disabled members of society to reach their full potential. They are often denied full access to housing, services and employment opportunities.

B *Making your vote count can be difficult*

C *Why is it difficult to communicate?*

A

Disability often reduces access to services in urban areas

I know it's difficult to understand what I say, but it would be easier if people tried.

It's my muscles in my jaw and tongue that are affected, not my mind. That works as clearly as you are reading this.

And I don't care how many times you ask me to repeat myself. I'd rather you do that than just nod and pretend you understand. For all you know I might have just told you that you've got a face like a bulldog sucking a wasp. Not that I would.

The worst thing is when people just ignore me and look the other way. Schools, employers, local authorities, I've been ignored by them all.

And like everyone else with cerebral palsy, I'm tired of it.

So are the Spastics Society. That's why they changed to Scope. Because it's about time that everyone with celebral palsy, however severely disabled, was allowed the scope to live normally. Which means not having our rights and abilities ignored.

Cerebral palsy often impairs the ability to communicate. Yours, not mine.

SCOPE
FOR PEOPLE WITH CEREBRAL PALSY
Formerly The Spastics Society

1 What do you understand by the term 'disabled'? Give some examples.

2 Look at **Source A**.
a For two scenes which show a disabled person experiencing difficulties:
   (i) describe the disability. State whether it is likely to be temporary or permanent
   (ii) describe the difficulty being experienced
   (iii) suggest solutions to the difficulty.
b Discuss other permanent and temporary disabilities. What difficulties may an urban environment create for them?

3 Look at **Sources B** and **C**. What message do they send about the ways in which people with disabilities are treated?

Who plans for disability?

How can a person who has not experienced a difficulty hope to create an environment which solves the problem? People working in Coventry tried to look at the ways in which wheelchair users experienced the urban environment. In this study, planners and wheelchair users worked together to identify the problems. They attempted three exercises:

1 drawing maps of routes taken between different parts of the city centre
2 identifying parts of the city considered accessible and inaccessible by wheelchair users
3 making a list of barriers to people in wheelchairs.

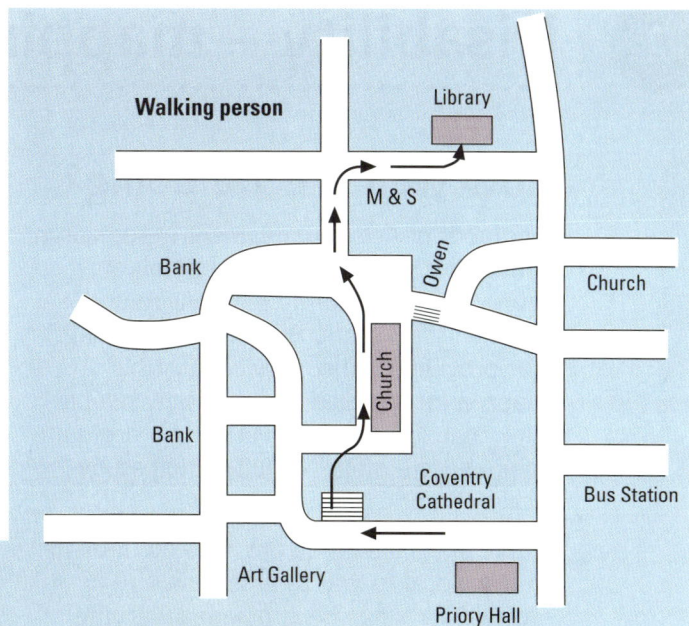

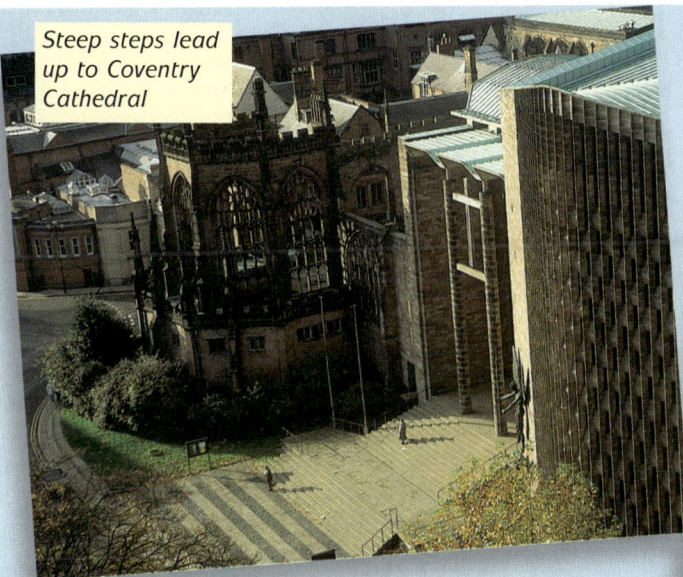

Walking person

Library
M & S
Bank
Owen
Church
Church
Bank
Coventry Cathedral
Bus Station
Art Gallery
Priory Hall

Steep steps lead up to Coventry Cathedral

Kerbs and cobbled streets also pose problems

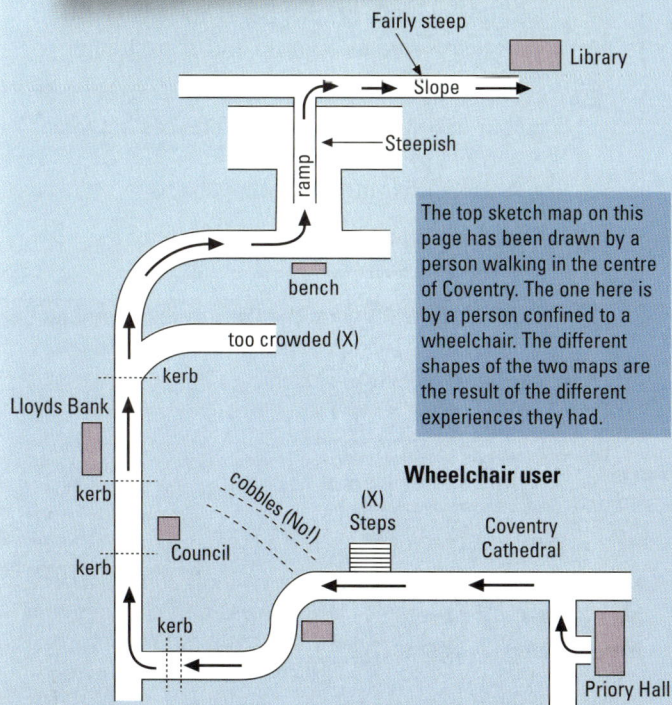

Fairly steep
Library
Slope
Steepish
ramp
bench
too crowded (X)
kerb
Lloyds Bank
kerb
cobbles (No!)
(X) Steps
Coventry Cathedral
Council
kerb
kerb
Priory Hall

Wheelchair user

The top sketch map on this page has been drawn by a person walking in the centre of Coventry. The one here is by a person confined to a wheelchair. The different shapes of the two maps are the result of the different experiences they had.

D Life can be difficult at times

4 Look at **Source D**.
   a Describe the route taken by the person walking between Priory Hall and the Library.
   b How is the wheelchair user's route different?
   c Name **three** barriers to the wheelchair user. Explain why each route could not be used.
   d In what ways could these difficulties be improved upon?

5 'People are not handicapped by their disabilities but by the way in which society as a whole treats them.' To what extent do you agree with the statement?

2 Disability – mapping access

How well are we doing?

A number of Acts of Parliament were passed during the 1990s with the intention of improving access to the built environment for wheelchair users. By 2004 all buildings that provide a public service must be adapted for disabled access. Many people think that these Acts of Parliament are quite weak and are often not fully enforced by local authorities.

In this assignment you are asked to look at an area local to you to assess how successfully it has been planned with the wheelchair user in mind. It may be possible for you to spend a short time in a wheelchair. It is definitely possible for all of you to map the difficulties posed by the built environment and the features that have been put in place to improve access for the wheelchair user.

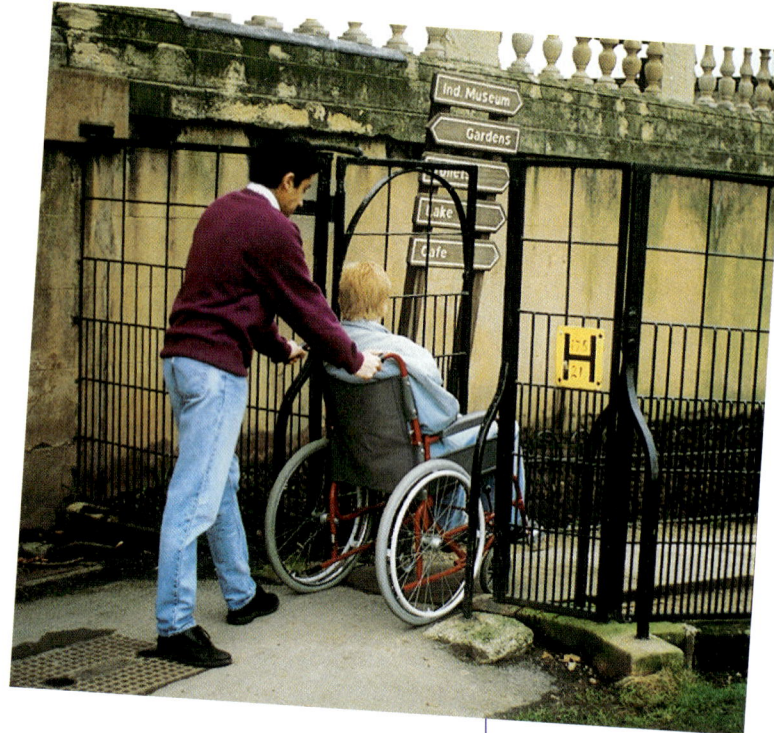

A *Experiencing the local environment*

B *Map symbols for use in assessing wheelchair access*

Surfaces

Smooth · Semi-rough · Rough · Gradient *(arrows in direction of slope)* · Gradient/Semi rough · Gradient/Rough · Tactile surface · No path

Parking/Crossing

Designated space	Ⓓ
Undesignated space	Ⓟ
Dishing	
Dishing/Lip	
No dishing	
Pedestrian Crossing (Zebra)	▮▮▮▮
Audio (with timer)	
Dishing but no crossing	
No dishing/No crossing	

On Pavement

		Disabled	Non-Disabled
	Unisex	Ⓤ	
Toilets	Female	Ⓕ	●
	Male	Ⓜ	
Telephone		T	⊠
Post Box		PB	PB
Bank ATM		£	
Street furniture		ⓘ	
Seat		Ⓢ	
Steps (with number)			
Ramp		►	
Ramp (with handrail)		▻	
Narrow footpath			
Big kerb			
Rail			

Off-Pavement

	Good	With lip	With steps	Steps inside	Steps or lip outside/steps inside
Single swing door					
Double swing door					
Narrow door					
Double narrow door					
Electric door					

The symbols show barriers to access and changes that have been put in place to increase accessibility

1. Agree the boundaries of an area close to your home or school to be assessed.

2. Survey each street within the area using a map and the symbols on this page. You may wish to collect the data as a group and share it later.

3. Create a final map of the area with the symbols colour keyed to show the differences between:
   • barriers to access
   • features that increase accessibility.

4. Comment on the area's accessibility to wheelchair users.

5. Outline a strategy for the future development of the area, paying particular attention to the needs of wheelchair users.

Urban-rural interaction

The 11 National Parks of England and Wales with the year of their creation. In 2001 both The South Downs and The New Forest were awaiting approval to be designated National Parks

Northumberland
NATIONAL PARK
(1956)

PEAK
DISTRICT
NATIONAL PARK
(1951)

Lake District
National Park
(1951)

YORKSHIRE DALES
National Park Authority
(1954)

(1951)

PARC CENEDLAETHOL ERYRI
SNOWDONIA
NATIONAL PARK

NORTH YORK MOORS
NATIONAL PARK
(1952)

KEY IDEAS

The population structure of urban and rural areas is dynamic and reflects physical, historical, social, economic and cultural influences.

Urbanization and counter-urbanization are taking place in different parts of the world for a variety of reasons.

Migration has a significant impact on the migrants and origins and destinations.

Increased short- and long-term access to and interaction between urban and rural areas is causing conflict and issues for sustainability.

New Forest

South Downs

Broads Authority
(1989)

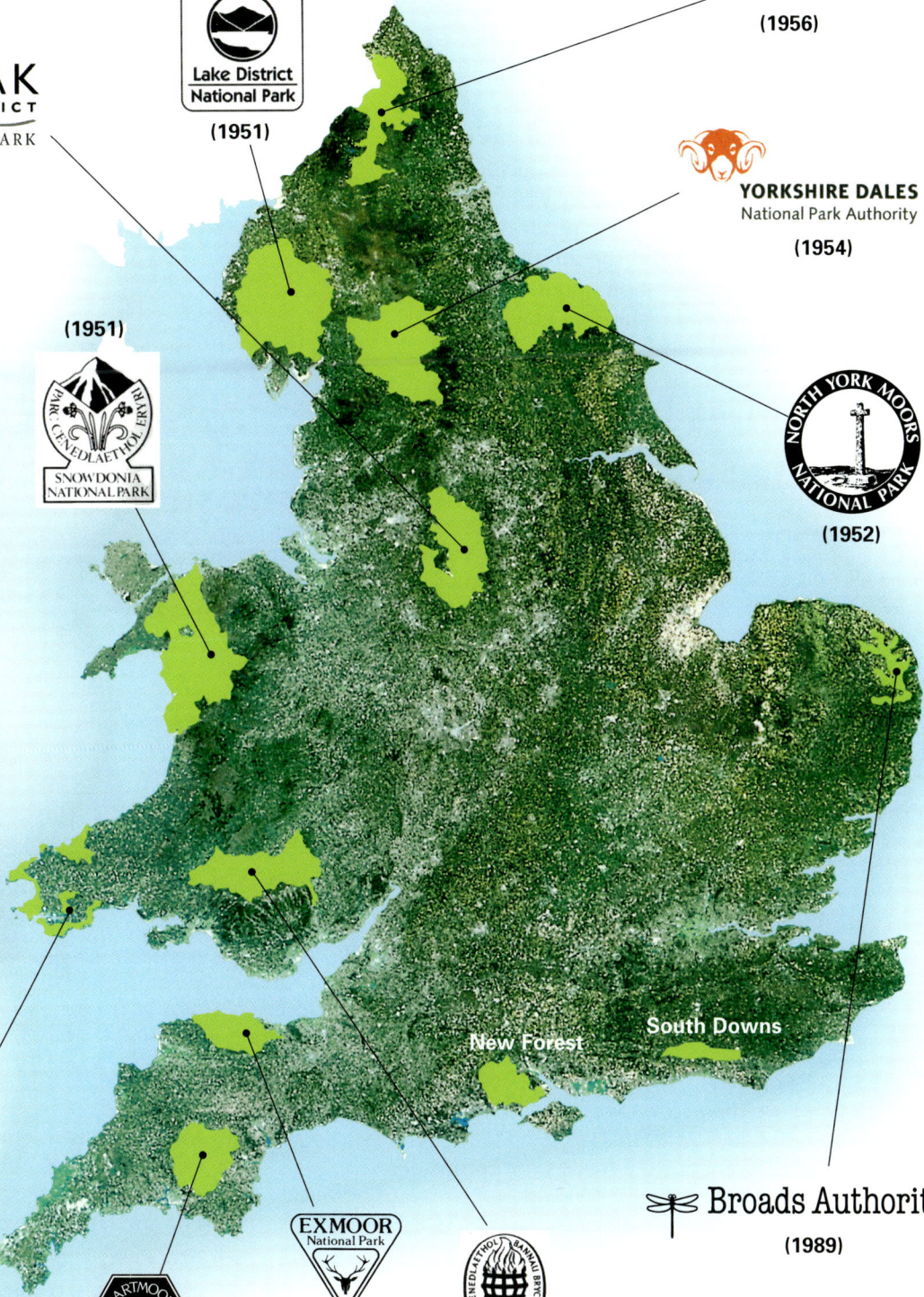

Parc Cenedlaethol Arfordir Penfro
Pembrokeshire Coast National Park
(1952)

DARTMOOR
NATIONAL PARK
(1952)

EXMOOR
National Park
(1954)

PARC CENEDLAETHOL BANNAU BRYCHEINIOG
BRECON BEACONS
NATIONAL PARK
(1957)

Why are people migrating into urban areas in LEDCs?

What are the effects of this movement on the areas they leave?

3.1 Moving into cities

The push of the countryside...

In most Less Economically Developed Countries (LEDCs) there is a movement of **migrants** from rural areas (countryside) into urban areas (the towns and cities.) The reasons for this **urbanization** can be divided into push factors and pull factors.

Push factors are those features of the countryside that make a person's quality of life so poor that they wish to move away. It could be the result of something that has affected the area for a long time, like poor education opportunities, or could be the result of a major disaster such as a flood.

A *Comparing poverty in regions of the world*

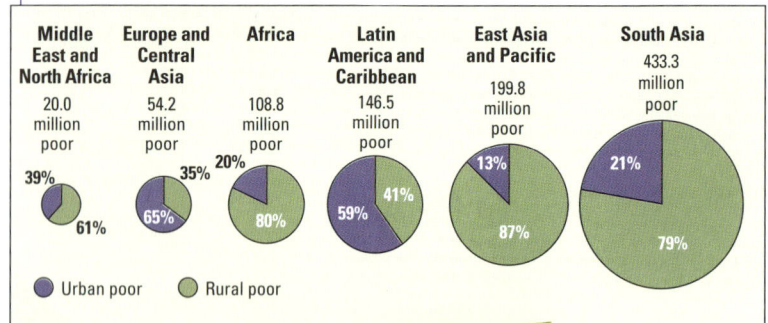

Middle East and North Africa	Europe and Central Asia	Africa	Latin America and Caribbean	East Asia and Pacific	South Asia
20.0 million poor	54.2 million poor	108.8 million poor	146.5 million poor	199.8 million poor	433.3 million poor
39% / 61%	35% / 65%	20% / 80%	41% / 59%	13% / 87%	21% / 79%

● Urban poor   ● Rural poor

C *Many children work in the fields of India's rural areas. There are few opportunities to attend school.*

B

Poverty drives Indian farmers to suicide

Poverty and hardship are not new in rural India where most of the 320 million people classified as 'living below the poverty line' live. In recent months, an estimated 300 cotton farmers in Andhra Pradesh killed themselves by consuming pesticides after they were hounded by India's worst pests – greedy moneylenders – waiting to foreclose mortgages on the farms.
A similar situation now faces cotton growers in Maharashtra state who have suffered from failed monsoons, moneylenders and falling cotton prices manipulated by dealers. In Karnataka, news reports say suicides have been recorded in the four northern states of Bihar, Gulbarga, Raichur and Dharwar following the failure of pulse crops. The lack of rain and a decrepit irrigation system have contributed to the woes of farmers here. Now there is a new menace causing the complete destruction of Karnataka's pulse crops – the dreaded borer pest against which, ironically, there are no effective pesticides to be found.

Adapted from a world news article from the Inter Press Service

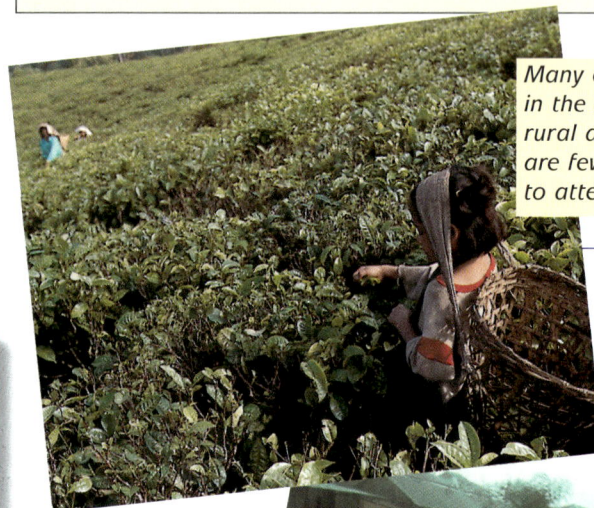

D *Flooding in the summer of the year 2000 killed over 2500 people, submerged tens of thousands of villages and destroyed more than 4 million hectares of crops.*

1 Look at **Source A**.
a What are the percentages of rural poor and urban poor in South Asia?
b How different are the figures for Europe and Central Asia?
c Rank the regions of the world according to the percentages of rural poor. Comment on your findings.

2 Study **Source B**. It is a news report about India, an LEDC.
a Make a list of factors from the report that might persuade people to migrate from the countryside to a city.
b For each factor, explain why it may encourage migration.

3 a Describe the scenes in **Sources C** and **D**.
b What push factors do these scenes illustrate?

...the pull of the city

Pull factors are often the opposite of push factors. For example, where opportunities for education are seen as being very poor in rural areas, people think that there will be a much greater chance of getting children into a school in the cities. It is this perception of a better quality of life that attracts people to cities. For many people arriving in the city, though, the reality is different and they are forced to live in shanty settlements like Sanjay Gandhi Nagar (see pages 24-27).

E

The percentage of households in India with the following facilities...

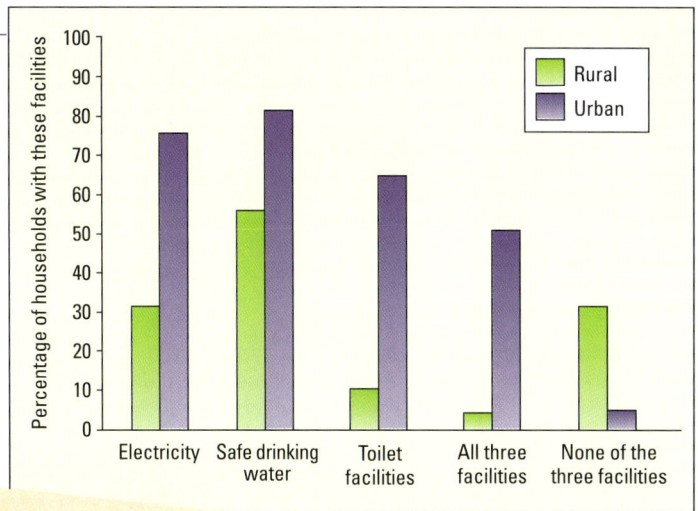

Source: Census 1991

F *Images of Mumbai, India*

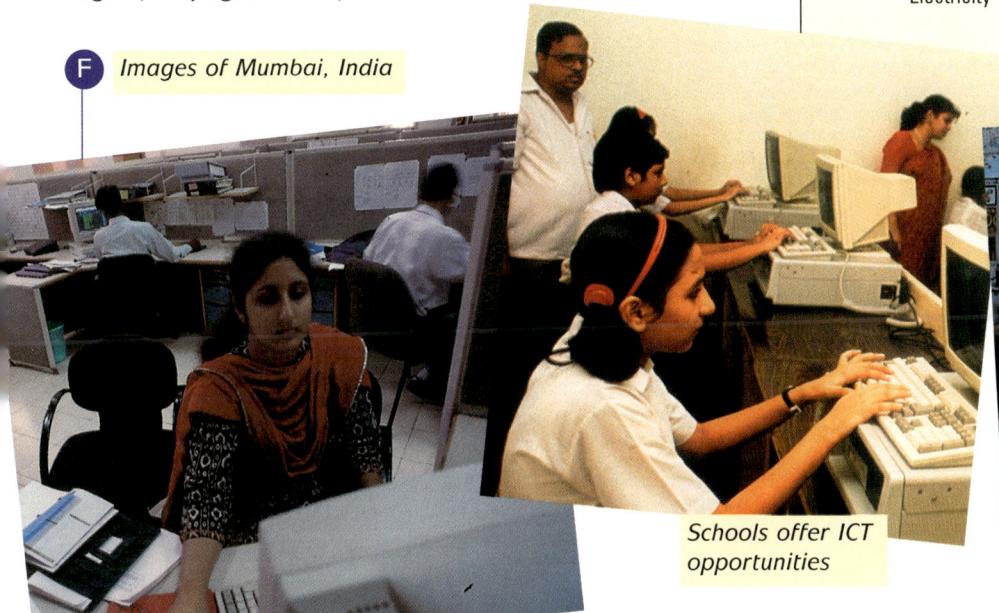

Working at Decibells Electronics Ltd

Schools offer ICT opportunities

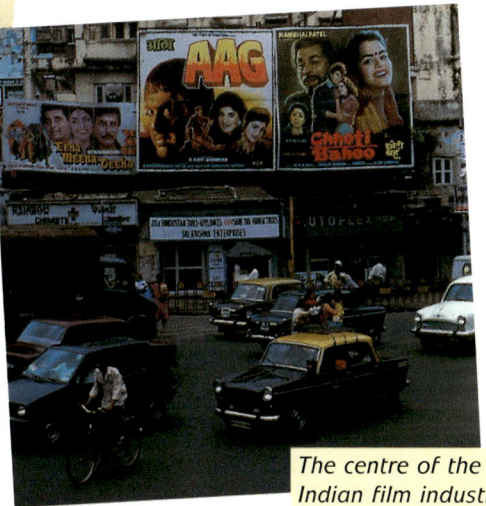

The centre of the Indian film industry

Effects on the countryside

If many people move into an urban area it can place a tremendous strain on the authorities and their attempts to provide housing and services for the inhabitants.
The effects are also seen, though, in the countryside where the people have come from. Usually the people who migrate are men between the ages of 15 and 45. This splits up families but, if the family goes too, it can have an even more severe effect. Often the elderly people who are left in the countryside are those who are least able to look after themselves.

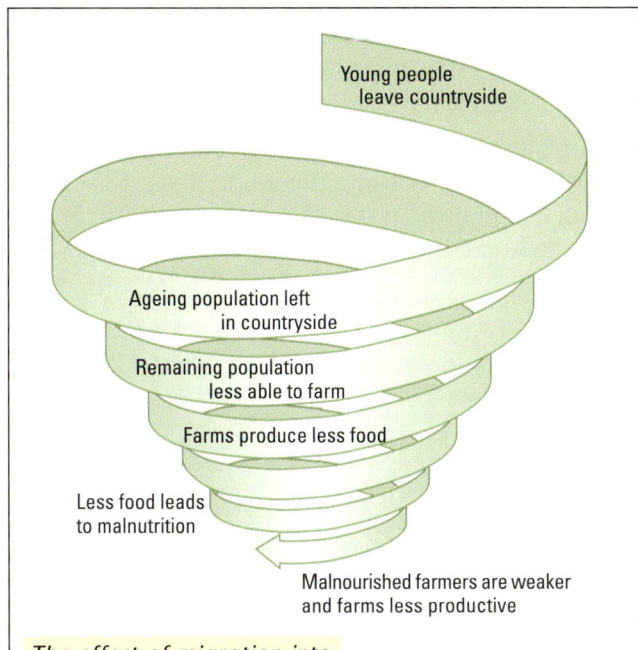

G

Young people leave countryside

Ageing population left in countryside

Remaining population less able to farm

Farms produce less food

Less food leads to malnutrition

Malnourished farmers are weaker and farms less productive

The effect of migration into cities on rural communities

4 Study **Source E**.
  a Describe the differences shown in the provision of facilities between rural and urban India.
  b Explain how these differences encourage people to migrate to the cities.
  c Are these push or pull factors? Explain your answer.

5 a Describe the scenes in **Source F**.
  b Suggest why each photo might attract people to Mumbai.

6 Imagine you are an old farmer whose children have migrated to the city. Use **Source G** to help you to persuade them to return to the village.

3.2 Developing the countryside

A *Mahad Taluka – the natural environment*

The main river, the Savitri, flows into the Arabian Sea. It has three main tributaries. These are dry between October and June.

The soils are permeable and do not retain much moisture. Those on the slopes are grassed while on the flatter land, closer to the coast, coconuts, betel nuts and rice can be grown.

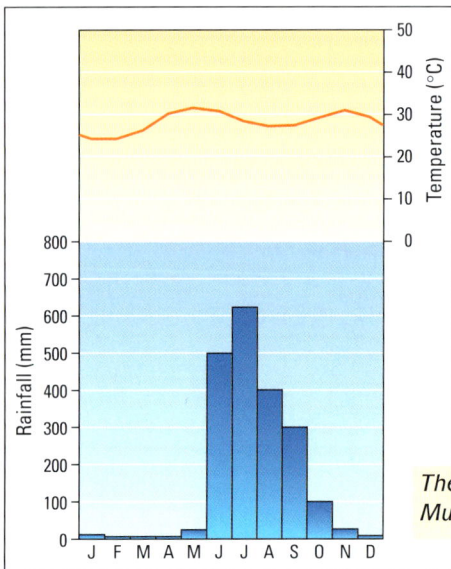

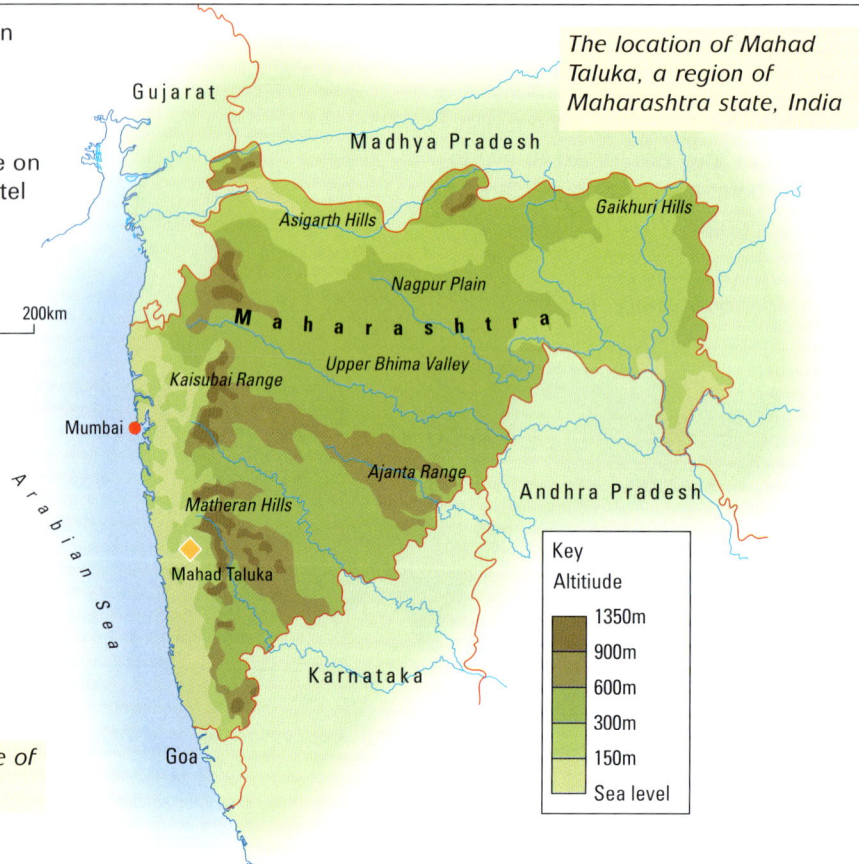

The location of Mahad Taluka, a region of Maharashtra state, India

Gujarat

Madhya Pradesh

Asigarth Hills

Gaikhuri Hills

Nagpur Plain

M a h a r a s h t r a

Upper Bhima Valley

Kaisubai Range

Mumbai

Ajanta Range

A n d h r a   P r a d e s h

Matheran Hills

Mahad Taluka

Karnataka

Goa

A r a b i a n   S e a

N

0   200km

Key
Altitiude

- 1350m
- 900m
- 600m
- 300m
- 150m
- Sea level

The climate of Mumbai

Temperature (°C)

Rainfall (mm)

J F M A M J J A S O N D

B *Mahad Taluka – the people*

- infant mortality is 25%
- almost half the population is under 14 years old
- over 45% of the 200 000 people are landless
- 70% of the people are illiterate
- 50% live below India's poverty level, with 78% in extreme poverty
- over 70% of the people are farmers
- 87% of the farmers own less than 2 hectares of land

In the villages, women do most of the work. Their husbands have left to find work in the cities. Women must raise the children and carry out domestic work as well as farm the land.

Poverty causes migration

The numbers of people who have migrated from the countryside to urban areas in LEDCs has placed a great strain on the cities they have moved into. They have also had a negative effect on the areas they have left.

Many reasons are given for the migration of people from rural to urban areas. The underlying fact is that most have their origins in poverty. The World Bank defines the poor as being people with incomes of less than $1 a day ($1 = approx. 70p). In India there are over 525 million people who live on less than $1 a day. Most of these are in the countryside.

If people are to be persuaded to stay in or return to the countryside, the living conditions and opportunities must be improved within the villages. Mahad Taluka is a rural region of India where improvements are taking place.

1 Use the map in **Source A** to help you describe the location of the region of Mahad Taluka.

2 a From **Sources A** and **B** describe the difficulties being faced by the people of Mahad Taluka. Use the following headings:
   (i) the natural environment
   (ii) human issues.
   b Explain how each difficulty you have described might affect quality of life.

PRIDE in India – a case study

PRIDE, INDIA is a group for 'Planning Rural-Urban Integrated Development through Education'. It was set up to try to reduce the problem of mass migration from rural to urban areas in India. PRIDE helps local people to plan, organize and work through their training towards self-sufficiency and **sustainable** development of communities. PRIDE has developed a Special Education Centre in the slums of Mumbai and has also been working in 140 of the 167 villages in the rural area of Mahad Taluka, about 200km south of Mumbai.

Education

- Pre-school education centres have been set up in all villages for children from two and a half to five and a half years of age. Local people are trained as teachers.
- Study centres and special coaching classes provide teaching mainly in English, Maths and Science. 'Whispering walls' in the study centres contain important information about the subjects.
- Children are given money from an education fund. This has to be repaid later.
- Children who have far to travel to school are given bicycles.
- Nearly 160 adult education centres are being run with the help of the government to create literate adults.
- Libraries and book banks encourage children to read.

PRIDE has trained many teachers and has created two secondary schools that it has handed over to the local state authority to run.

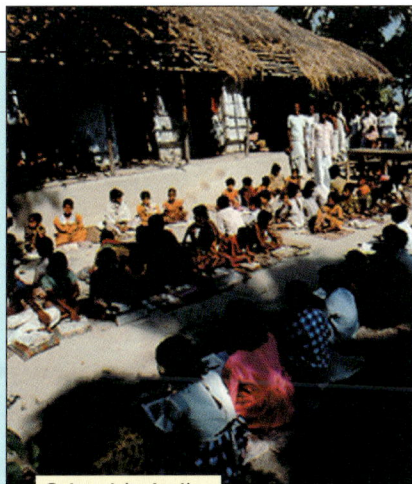

School in India

Community development

- Two hundred toilet blocks spread over 35 villages are being built.
- Villagers are encouraged to use smokeless stoves and bio-gas plants.
- PRIDE has replanted many areas with new trees.
- The Mahali Mandal group allows women to come together at village level to work together to solve village problems.
- Separate youth clubs operate for girls and boys. They teach practical skills through voluntary work like improving village roads, village beautification and tree planting.

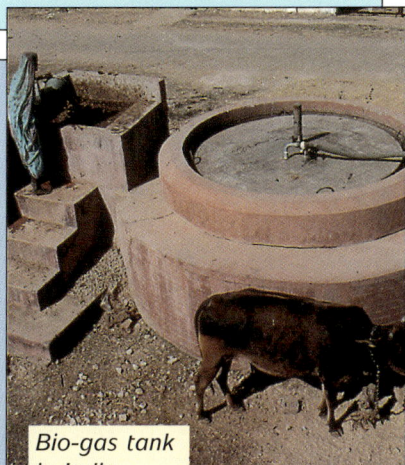

Bio-gas tank in India

C *The work of PRIDE*

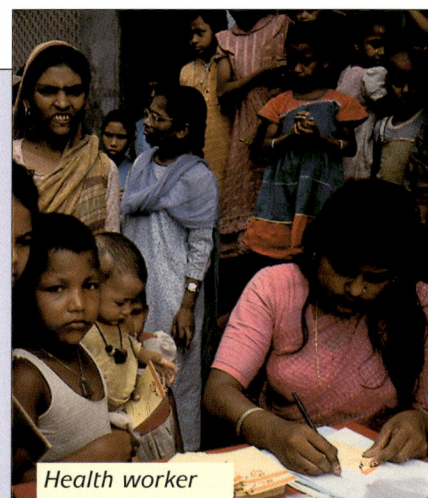

Health and nutrition

- Children under five are given Vitamin A to prevent diarrhoea and are immunised.
- The project travels around villages every three months using a mobile van donated by Australia.
- Great effort goes into the care of pregnant women and old people.
- Essential medicines are provided free of charge.
- Health workers are selected from the villagers and trained.
- Kitchen gardens are developed and nutritious recipes for children are prepared each day from local food.

Health worker visits rural areas

Economic development

PRIDE has worked with the national government to set up many schemes aimed at developing sustainable livelihoods to stop migration from the villages.

- Loans can be obtained through the Women's Credit Co-operative Society.
- A farmers club, animal medical camps, milk pasteurising units, poultry units and plant nurseries have been set up
- The land is too rocky for simple boreholes, but irrigation schemes have been set up using check dams and reservoirs to raise the water table. Villagers have a supply of water for most of the year and tankers are used to supply those that still have a poor supply.
- Villagers can be trained at a centre running courses ranging from goat rearing to baking and tailoring.

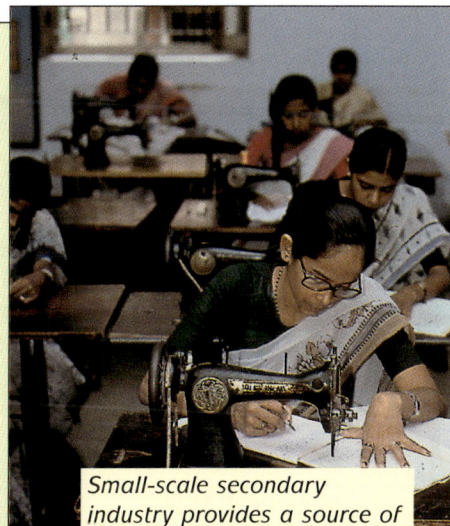

Small-scale secondary industry provides a source of income other than farming

3 Look at your answers to question 2. Use information from **Source C** to list the ways in which the work of PRIDE is overcoming each of the difficulties experienced by the people of Mahad Taluka.

4 Read the work on Sanjay Gandhi Nagar (pages 24-27). Where would you prefer to live: a village in Mahad Taluka or the Sanjay Gandhi Nagar settlement in Mumbai? Explain your answer.

Why do people migrate?
What patterns of migration exist?
What issues do asylum seekers raise?

3.3 People on the move

Migration – choice or no choice?

Many groups of people and individuals have chosen to migrate in order to take advantage of a more favourable area. They have left their home environment because they expect their new area to be more attractive and to offer more in terms of their lifestyle. Many of them expect to be financially better off. They are known as **economic migrants**.

Another group of migrants also exists. These people have fled or have been forced out of their home country because of war or foreign occupation, fear of religious, racial or political persecution, or because of natural disasters. People who fall into these groups are known as **refugees**.

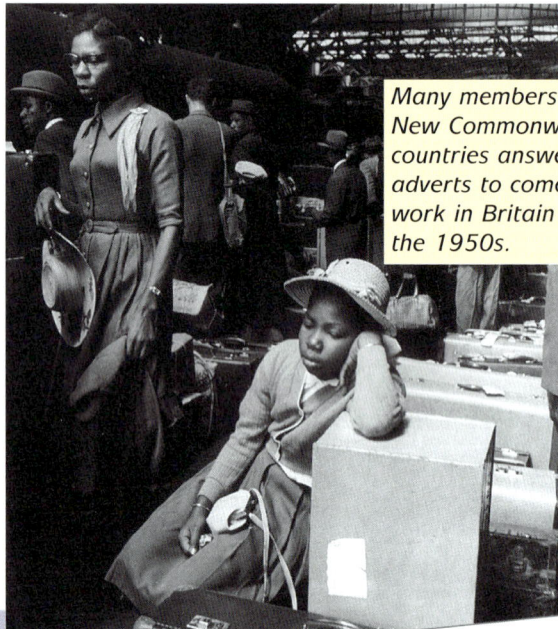

Many members of New Commonwealth countries answered adverts to come to work in Britain in the 1950s.

A

Sun Seekers
– a camp site near Marbella, Spain

The couple, in their sixties, have now been here for five years. After enjoying a package holiday in the area they flew home, collected their pension books and have been living in a static caravan ever since.

Collapse of Communism Increases Migrations

The changes in government between 1989 and 1991 in Eastern Europe have resulted in mass movements of people. As restrictions on movement were removed many migrated from east to west in Germany and there was a substantial movement of Jews from Russia to Israel.

More Sri Lankans move for work

Violence continues in Sri Lanka. The island, on the southern tip of India, continues to be in the grip of civil war. Protests and the terrorist bombing of houses and buses are combined with strikes and the imposition of curfews. Many people have moved from their homes and, in 1999, the numbers of people moving abroad for work rose by 12% on the previous year. Many of these gained employment in India.

USA – A Country of Mass Asylum

Since 1946 the USA has accepted over one million refugees. They have fled political oppression in Cuba, Haiti and Indochina, amongst other areas.

1 Write a definition of each of the following terms:
- economic migrant
- refugee.

2 Look at **Source A**.
a   Use an atlas and an outline world map to arrow and label the migrations.
b   Discuss other twentieth century or more recent international migrations. Add these to your map.
c   Use symbols to identify each migration as either 'economic' or 'refugee' or 'other'. Justify these decisions.

IRAQIS FORCED OUT BY PERSECUTION

Over half a million Iraqis now take shelter in south-west Iran. They are, for the most part, victims of the Iraqi regime's repression following the 1991 Gulf War. They had suffered arrest, detention, torture and also the napalm bombing and poisoning of their home areas. They are isolated and trapped. They want to return home but that is not an option at present.

B *Applications of asylum seekers to European countries*

Country	Number (Jan–Oct 2000)	% change (Jan–Oct 1999/2000)
UK	80 730	+9
Germany	64 890	–20
Belgium	38 295	+20
France	36 665	+30
Netherlands	36 295	+15
Austria	15 090	–10
Switzerland	14 420	–66
Sweden	11 650	+28
Ireland	9 080	+65
Denmark	8 655	+69
Norway	6 280	–26
Spain	6 020	–17
Finland	2 835	+20
Greece	2 075	+36
Luxembourg	445	–84
Portugal	160	+40
Italy	Not yet available	

Source: *The Times*, 26 January 2001

D *Some views of people against asylum seekers coming to the UK*

1 Britain is a soft touch and takes more than its fair share.
2 Most asylum seekers come from safe countries.
3 Only a small proportion of refugees are genuine.
4 Asylum seekers get massive state handouts.
5 Asylum seekers are taking our housing.
6 Council tax is going up to fund asylum seekers.
7 Asylum seekers are taking UK jobs.

Welcome to Britain?

There are more than 33 million people who have had to leave their homes because of war. Of these, over fourteen million have crossed international borders to flee their former lives. Nine million of these have fled from just five conflicts in Rwanda, Liberia, Afghanistan, Palestine and former Yugoslavia. Between January and October 2000, over 80 000 **asylum seekers** applied to come to Britain. Many came across the English Channel and are temporarily being housed in Kent.

'Britain is too conscious about being unbiased towards these people; that is actually way too lax! We should sort out our own people before helping others!'

C *Different views*

'Developed countries such as the UK should keep an open door to those people in less privileged countries who are being persecuted because of their political, religious or economic beliefs. If this door is shut, the world's problems would increase rapidly.'

E *Views of the charity Oxfam*

a Most refugees coming to the UK are from the former Yugoslavia, Somalia, Sri Lanka, Afghanistan, Colombia, Turkey, Iraq and Iran. These are all countries with serious conflict or a grave human rights record.

b Asylum seekers are mainly being housed in 'hard-to-let' accommodation that people on council waiting lists don't want.

c During 1999, around 47% of asylum seekers were allowed to remain and another 10% to 20% were generally successful on appeal. There were also some that appeared to be rejected unfairly.

d The costs of looking after asylum seekers are met by central government. The Home Office estimates that it will spend £300 million in 2000-2001. Much of the cost is because applications take a long time to process.

e Asylum seekers are legally unable to work for the first six months. Even when they can work they find it difficult due to language problems, lack of training and lack of transport.

f An asylum-seeking couple is given £57.37 per week in vouchers. £10 of these can be converted into cash and the rest must be used in designated shops.

g Although the UK has the largest number of applications from asylum seekers, when compared to its population size, it is only ranked 8th in the top 17 European countries.

F

Refugees make the headlines in Dover, Kent in 1997

3 Study **Source B**.
a What is an 'asylum seeker'?
b On an outline map of European Union countries, use a choropleth shading system to show the number of applications received by each country.
c Compare the percentage change in applications since January 1999 for the UK and Germany. Comment on your findings.

4 a List reasons why asylum seekers leave their home countries.
b Suggest why some people who are not being persecuted might pretend to be asylum seekers.
c Explain why governments require asylum seekers to apply to stay in their new country.

5 Study **Sources C, D** and **E**.
a Match the statements in **Source D** with those in **Source E**.
b Suggest why people have different opinions about asylum seekers.
c What is your view about genuine asylum seekers who want to live in the UK?

6 a Discuss your feelings towards the scene in **Source F**.
b Outline a plan for integrating asylum seekers with other members of their new community.

3.4 A breath of fresh air

How did the population of St. Kilda reflect environmental, historical, social, economic and cultural influences?

What caused the population to change?

How was the quality of life affected by the population change?

A

The location of St Kilda

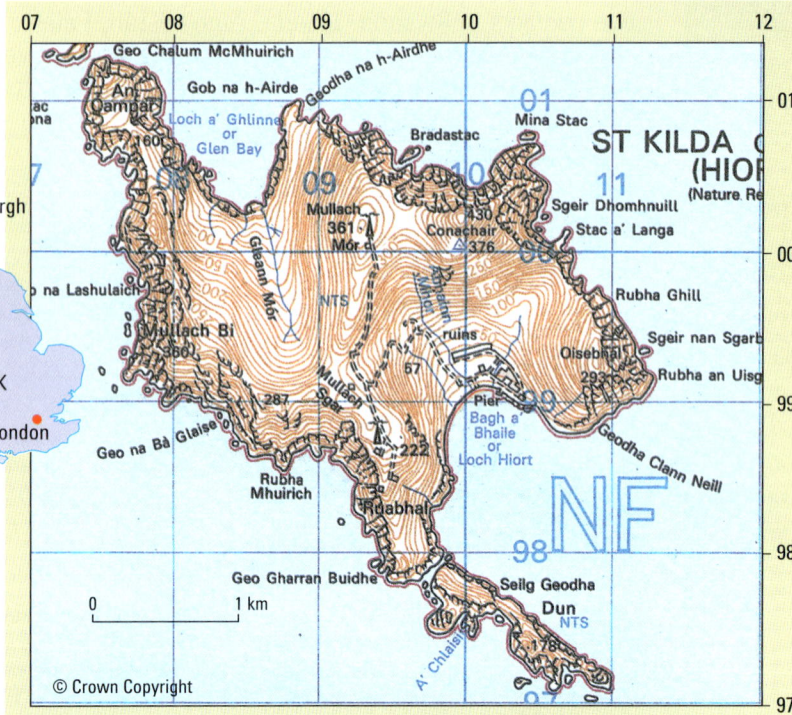

Challenging weather and climate!

With gusts of 209 km per hour it is the windiest place in the British Isles. Sheep can be lifted off their hooves! It can rain for 2-3 weeks without stopping. However in late summer there are long sunny days because of the northerly location. Getting to St. Kilda is a challenge in itself. On a good day it takes 6 hours by boat from Harris; in rough seas ships have been lost.

B Oblique photo of Village Bay or Bagh a' Bhaile

The good life?

Migrating from rural areas to urban areas or from one country to another are not new issues. You may never have heard of St. Kilda (*Hirta* in Gaelic). It rarely appears on maps, yet evidence shows that this isolated rural environment was settled for over 4000 years. The 1851 census revealed a **self-sufficient** community of 180 people. From the mid-nineteenth century there were increasing links with the Scottish mainland. With better opportunities offered in industrial cities like Glasgow, the Western Islands of Scotland began to suffer from depopulation. None was affected more than the island of St. Kilda.

1 Study **Source A** and an atlas.
   a Estimate the distance and give the direction of St. Kilda from Harris?
   b Estimate the distance in kilometres from Glasgow and your own home to St. Kilda.
   c List evidence that shows that St. Kilda is a remote and isolated part of the UK.

2 Study **Sources A** and **B**.
   a Estimate the area of St. Kilda in square kilometres.
   b Locate and name the highest point on the island. Use a six-figure grid reference.
   c Use **Source A** to help you decide from which direction **Source B** was taken.
   d Suggest which **two** grid squares on the map contain most of the land in the photograph.

Life on St. Kilda

St. Kilda was owned by the Macleods of Skye. The mainstay of the self-sufficient community was the rented croft, a single storey thatched cottage with a hectare of land around it. The tenants kept sheep and cattle on the holding during winter then for the rest of the year let them graze over the moorlands while oats and barley were grown close to the house. Manure from animals and seaweed added nutrients to the thin, impermeable soils. Granite stones were used to grind oats for porridge. Tools were limited to penknives for sheep shearing, spades for digging and rakes for removing stones. Fishing took place only in summer to avoid disturbing bird's nests. Bird fowling was essential for survival with boiled seabird a staple part of the diet. Nothing was wasted. Beaks were used as roof-nails, feathers sold for pillows and oil was used for heat and light.

Survival in such an enclosed community relied on co-operation. The men held 'parliaments' each morning to plan the day's work. All the resources were shared and the elderly and sick catered for. Women were more concerned with child rearing, weaving and spinning, tending animals and harvesting the crops. They also developed much of St. Kilda's culture with Gaelic songs and poetry heard at 'ceilidhs'.

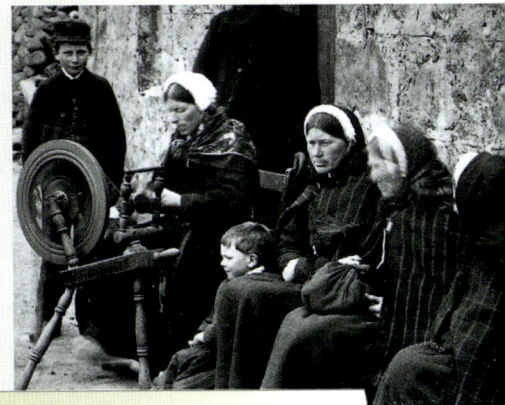

We the undersigned natives of St. Kilda hereby respectfully pray and petition HM Government to assist us to leave the island this year and to find homes and occupations on the mainland...

On 10 May, 1930 the islanders wrote to the Prime Minister, Ramsay Macdonald

E *The island was given to the National Trust for Scotland in 1954. Today ornithologists, campers and tourists visit St Kilda.*

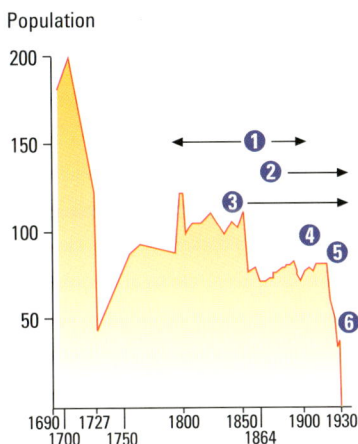

The leaving of St. Kilda

1 In the nineteenth century men left for better prospects in industrial Glasgow.

2 From 1852, 36 people emigrated to Australia.

3 Between 1830 and 1930 birth rates fell below death rates and the number of marriages fell. The population began to age as it lost its young people, especially its men.

4 Men who survived the First World War (1914-1918) failed to return to St. Kilda. They had seen better prospects elsewhere.

5 From 1920 more frequent calls by ships, and media developments such as VHF Radio broadened the islanders' horizons.

6 The winter of 1929-1930 was the worst on record. There was no mainland contact from August to March. Food was running out. The 36 people who were left had had enough.

Population graph — vertical axis Population: 200, 150, 100, 50; horizontal axis: 1690, 1700, 1727, 1750, 1800, 1850, 1864, 1900, 1930. Markers ①②③④⑤⑥

The National Trust for Scotland

ST KILDA
WORK PARTIES 2000

D *The death of St. Kilda*

3 Survival on St. Kilda meant making the most of the natural resources through the skill and enterprise of the people.
  a Use **Source C** to help you decide how the islanders provided:
   • different types of food
   • clothing
   • housing and shelter for people and animals.
  b Suggest why this way of life was sustainable for thousands of years.
  c Describe the different contributions of men and women to the economic, social and cultural life of St. Kilda.

4 Study **Source D**.
  a Describe the changes in population between 1700 and 1930.
  b Produce a diary of events that caused the population to change.
  c Suggest how these changes affected the quality of life for different groups of people who:
   • stayed on the island • left the island.
  d How do you think the 36 islanders felt when they were evacuated in 1930?

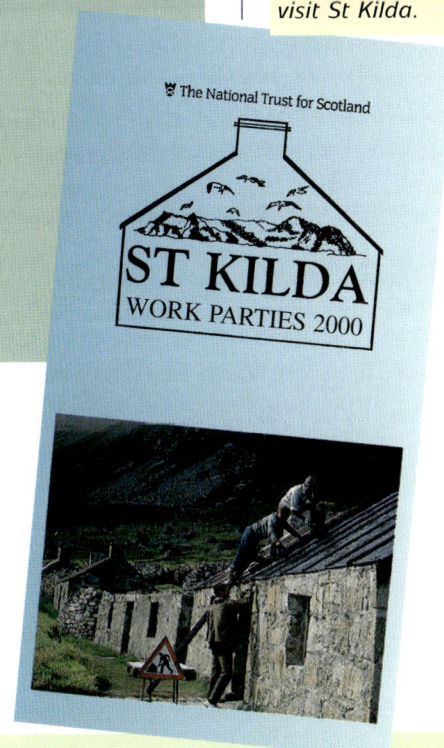

5 Study **Source E**.
  a Who owns St. Kilda today?
  b Which groups of people visit the island? Why do they go?
  c Plan a short holiday on St. Kilda.
   (i) Use an atlas to describe the route from your home.
   (ii) Describe two days' activities that you would want to carry out.

3.5 Keeping people in a difficult region

The Western Isles

The reasons for people leaving St. Kilda are similar for much of the Western Islands and the Highlands and Islands Region of Scotland. By the mid-1960s, few of the people who remained wanted to live there. Cities such as Glasgow had emptied the glens of young people, leaving ageing communities unable to cope. Something had to be done to attract people back into the region and a way of life that was sustainable.

In 1965 the *Highlands and Islands Development Board* (HIDB) was created. In 1991 it became the *Highlands and Islands Enterprise* (HIE) with ten regions covering the north of Scotland. In this time both groups have used **private** and **public sector** money plus grants from the European Union (EU) to persuade people not to move out of, and to attract people to, the north of Scotland. *Western Isles Enterprise* is one of the ten HIE regions.

The Skye Bridge, costing £25 million, was opened in September 1995. It links the mainland with Skye and will improve access to the Western Isles by reducing travel time to Uig and Broadford Airport.

Average journey times by car

From	To Glasgow	To Edinburgh
Inverness	3hrs	2hrs 45 mins
Fort William	2hrs	2hrs 25 mins

Roll-on-roll-off ferries

Ullapool/Stornoway	3hrs 40min
Oban/Barra	5hrs

Flying times from Inverness

Glasgow	45 mins
London (Heathrow)	1hr 45 mins
Stornoway	40 mins

A

The Western Isles

Key
Airports
— Air routes
◈ Telecottages
▬ Major ferry routes
— Major roads
○ Small settlements

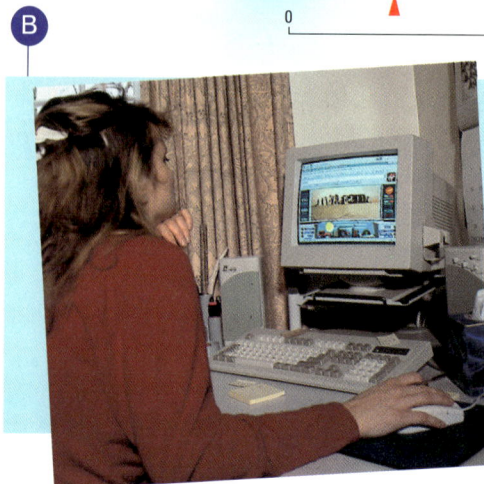

1 Access from the mainland to the Western Isles was a major problem in the past.

a On an outline copy of the map from **Source A** show the main access routes to and on the Western Isles today. Include:
 • ferry routes
 • roads
 • air routes
 • bridges.

b Use examples to explain how different routes marked on your map have improved the accessibility of the Western Isles to mainlanders.

2 Study **Sources A** and **B**.

a Add the tele-cottages to your outline map.

b What is a 'tele-worker'? Suggest which types of occupation suit 'tele-working'.

c Suggest why these people prefer to work from the Western Isles. What disadvantages are there?

B

Live Local, Work Global: Tele-cottages are small centres providing access to computer technology, desktop–publishing and global information through the internet. They allow people to live and work on the islands while sharing access to telecommunications and IT with other 'tele-workers'.

The Highland Strategy

'The Western Isles Enterprise recognises that our greatest resource in these islands is our people and that we are committed to making an environment conducive to business investment. This, and an excellent quality of lifestyle, will set these islands apart as the location in which to live and to work.'

Agnes Rennie, Chairwoman of WIE until 1999

AIM
TO ENABLE THE PEOPLE OF THE HIGHLANDS AND ISLANDS TO REALISE THEIR FULL POTENTIAL

Iomairt nan Eilean Siar
Western Isles
ENTERPRISE

Highlands & Islands
ENTERPRISE

DEVELOPING SKILLS

ENVIRONMENT

CULTURE

GROWING BUSINESSES

STRENGTHENING COMMUNITIES

The Stolt Sea Farms factory

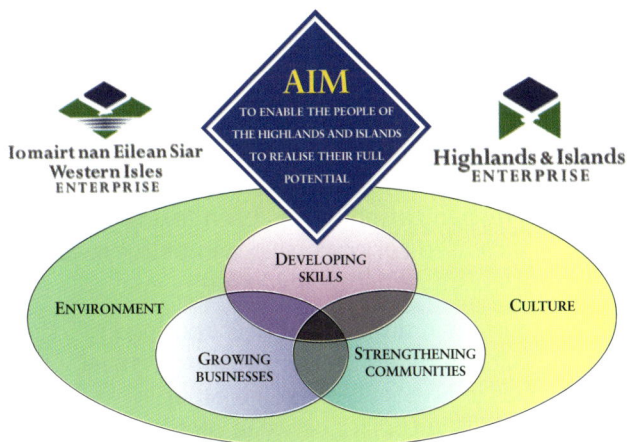

'1999 has been a difficult year for many traditional industries. The strength of the pound has had a serious effect on the export of Harris Tweed, shellfish and salmon. Visitor numbers are also down. High fuel and transport costs continue to be a major barrier to development in this area. However developing ICT activities and the University of the Highlands and Islands has prevented the drift of highly qualified islanders to the mainland.'

Duncan Maciness, Chairman of WIE since 1999

Growing businesses ... work began in 1999 on the WIE's biggest project, the Stolt Sea Farms factory in Scalpay. Costing over £4 million, the factory will process salmon from local fish farms and provide 109 jobs.

Strengthening communities ... a Community Action Grant of £3000 for play area equipment went to Taigh Sgoile, Dhunsgealair, a community resource for the Sollas area of North Uist.

Developing skills ... the University of the Highlands and Islands continues to expand across HIE areas. The Cisco ICT firm was attracted to Stornoway by the UHIE and provides ICT training and expertise. Today at least twenty island firms are involved in e-commerce dealings.

C The work of the Western Isles Enterprise (WIE)

3 Study **Source C**.
a Suggest why the Western Isles symbol is shown in two languages.
b Why does the Chairman say that 1999 was a difficult year? What are his hopes for the future?

4 Study **Source D**.
a Describe the population changes in the HIDB area from 1851 to 1961.
b How successful has the HIDB and HIE been in holding and attracting population in the ten regions since 1961?

5 Read **Source E**.
a What evidence is there that people are still leaving the WIE area?
b Give reasons for the continuing out-migration.
c How has the lack of work affected Lachlan Macinnes and his family?

6 The Minister of Highlands and Islands has been asked to brief the Scottish Parliament on the work of the WIE. You are the Minister's researcher and have been asked to gather information under four headings:
• the aims of the WIE
• some examples of its successes
• current issues
• future hopes.
Your brief should be in note form and cover no more than two sides of A4 paper.

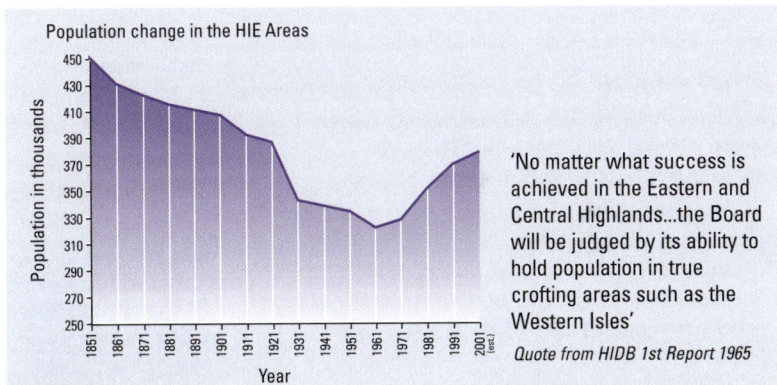

Population change in the HIE Areas

Population in thousands

'No matter what success is achieved in the Eastern and Central Highlands...the Board will be judged by its ability to hold population in true crofting areas such as the Western Isles'

Quote from HIDB 1st Report 1965

E Still work to do...

D Population change graph in the HIE area

Western Isles failing to hold population

Angus Graham, of the Western Isles Council, has watched with envy the success of the HIE in other areas of Scotland. "Inverness, Moray, Shetland, Orkney and Skye are booming – we are not" he says. In the last century population has fallen from 4 6 000 to 29 000. Demand for Harris Tweed is down; today there are only 150 weavers left. Trawlers are outnumbered five to one by the Spanish and French ships that fish off the west coasts of Lewis and Harris. Everyone agrees that the future depends on oil exploration and the multiplier effects of the oil industry around Stornoway if Texaco and Conoco discover oil.

LAST FERRY FROM LEWIS FOR ISLANDERS IN QUEST FOR STEADY JOBS

When his classmates left the Isle of Lewis to work in Inverness, Glasgow and Edinburgh, Lachlan Macinnes did anything and everything to stay on the Hebrides. First he was a soldier, then a gents' outfitter in Stornoway. Then he sold petrol before selling life insurance. Next month he will say farewell to his wife and three children and head for the mainland. It is fourteen months since he lost his insurance job and he cannot find another. He is about to become an economic migrant.

Sources adapted from
The Observer 8 March 1998

3.6 Who is the countryside for?

Why is counter-urbanization taking place in the UK?

What advantages and disadvantages can counter-urbanization bring to rural areas?

Counter-urbanization

While people in many LEDCs, such as India, and some parts of MEDCs, such as the Western Isles of Scotland, are migrating into urban areas, many towns and cities in MEDCs have people moving into rural areas. This movement of people out of urban areas is known as **counter-urbanization**. It has been taking place during the last 50 years due to increased car ownership and better roads. These allow people to commute to work, services and leisure.

There is now increased demand by urban dwellers for new housing in rural areas. In addition, people living in urban areas increasingly travel into rural areas for leisure activities in National Parks and other attractive environments. Today there is a conflict between preserving the quality of life in the countryside for those who live there and its use for new homes or pleasure by people who do not live there.

B *Urban sprawl 1991–2016*

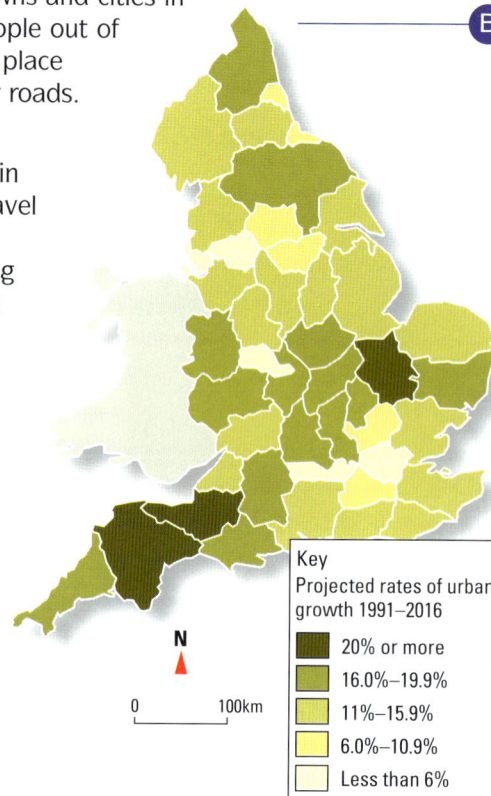

Key
Projected rates of urban growth 1991–2016

- 20% or more
- 16.0%–19.9%
- 11%–15.9%
- 6.0%–10.9%
- Less than 6%

N

0   100km

A *Trends in counter-urbanization*

	Population	1971	1981	1991	Change 1971-1991
England	Total	46 412	46 821	48 208	+1 796
	Percentage				+3.9%
Rural	Total	11 071	12 059	12 936	+1 865
	Percentage				+16.9%
Urban	Total	35 341	34 761	35 272	-69
	Percentage				-0.2%

Source: Office of Population Censuses and Surveys mid-year population estimates. Total figures are in thousands.

In-migration to rural areas continues. Between 1991 and 1997, over half a million more people moved from town to country. Many were from London and other **conurbations** but some were from New Towns like Milton Keynes.

Source: In-migration into rural England, The Countryside Agency, April 2000

C *The housing problem – new houses are needed in rural areas but many are built for commuters with money and are not affordable for young people from the village who now want their own house.*

British still seek rural dream...

Every day, 30 people abandon city life in Britain. Car exhausts, asthma, fear of crime, traffic jams and poor housing all combine to make urban life intolerable. In one survey, 81% of residents said they would prefer to have their home in a village or small English town.

Source: Robin McKie, The Observer, 26 May 1996

D *Where can we build new homes?*

We made mistakes in the 1960s by cramming people into hastily-built tower blocks. But we do not want to build on the green spaces in inner cities and remove playing fields and parks. Anyway, much of the vacant inner city land is contaminated by past industry. It is not suitable for new homes.

Tony Struthers of the Royal Town Planning Institute (RTPI)

We accept more homes are needed but the government should force planners to re-use derelict old inner city areas for new homes before looking at rural sites. Putting over four million new homes in the countryside is the equivalent of adding ten cities the size of Bristol. People are being pushed out rather than anything being done to improve cities. We must make cities more attractive places to live.

Council for Protection of Rural England (CPRE)

1 Study **Source A**.
  a How does the table show that counter-urbanization took place in the UK between 1971 and 1991?
  b What evidence suggests that in-migration to rural areas has continued since 1991?

2 Study **Source B**.
  a Use an atlas to list counties where urban growth will be more than 20% by 2016.
  b In which counties is urban growth expected to be less than 6%?
  c Suggest reasons for the growth patterns on the map.

3 Read **Source C**.
  a From the extract give **three** reasons why people want to leave the cities.
  b Add others to your list.

The figures show the predicted percentage growth of traffic on rural roads by the year 2025

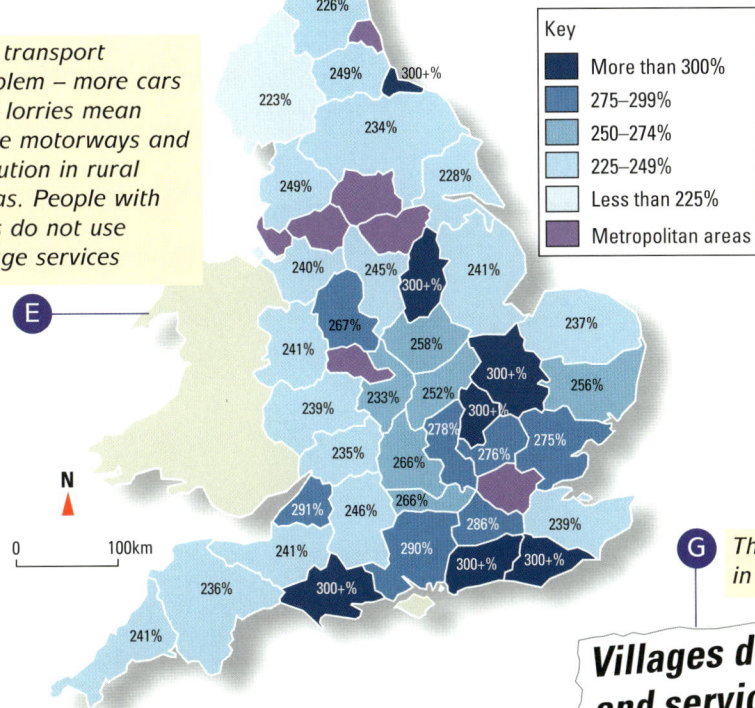

Key
- More than 300%
- 275–299%
- 250–274%
- 225–249%
- Less than 225%
- Metropolitan areas

The transport problem – more cars and lorries mean more motorways and pollution in rural areas. People with cars do not use village services

E

Map figures: 226%, 249%, 300+%, 223%, 234%, 228%, 249%, 240%, 245%, 300+%, 241%, 267%, 258%, 237%, 241%, 256%, 300+%, 239%, 233%, 252%, 278%, 300+%, 275%, 235%, 266%, 276%, 291%, 246%, 266%, 286%, 239%, 241%, 290%, 300+%, 300+%, 236%, 300+%, 241%

N

0 — 100km

The service problem – the Fosse Park Shopping Centre has been built by Junction 21 of the M1 motorway on the edge of Leicester. It has caused rural shops to close in nearby villages

F

G **The countryside in decline?**

Villages dying as shops and services close

Young people leave countryside through boredom and lack of cheap housing

Farmers better off using land for caravan sites

Golf courses and retail parks take up more rural

People feel strongly about the countryside (July 1997)

Wish list of improvements to village life	
1956	**1999**
1 Sewerage	1 Public transport
2 Street lighting	2 Slower speeds
3 Buses	3 Higher police presence
4 Bus shelter	4 New shop
5 Water	5 New village hall
6 Footpaths	6 Traffic calming
7 Village hall	7 Car parking facilities
8 Litter bins	8 Street lighting
9 Electricity	9 Youth facilities
10 Road improvements	10 Post office

Roll call of shutdown premises			
474	Post offices	70	Bakers
178	Pubs	58	Grocers
145	Banks or building societies	40	Hairdressers
98	Churches or chapels	36	Hardware shops
55	Surgeries	29	Mobile shops
196	Butchers	27	Haberdashers
71	Greengrocers	24	Newsagents

Source National Federation of Women's Institutes from The Times, 5 July 1999

4 Read **Source D**.
a Complete a copy of the table below.
b Add some views of your own.
c Should more housing be built in the countryside?

Building houses in the countryside	
Reasons FOR	Reasons AGAINST

5 Many people blame the increase in car ownership for rural problems. Study **Source E**.
a From the map, and using an atlas, list the counties which are expected to have at least a 300% increase in cars using rural roads in 2025.
b Describe the distribution of counties which will be least affected. Suggest why.
c Choose **two** English counties: one you know well and one contrasting county. Compare how each will be affected by the predictions shown in **Sources B** and **E**.

6 Look at the photo in **Source F**.
a What development is shown?
b Suggest why it is located close to a motorway junction and the edge of Leicester.
c Why might this development affect local village services in this area?

7 Study **Source G**.
a From the table list the top **three** and bottom **three** improvements wished for in 1956.
b Compare these with the list for 1999. Suggest reasons for the changes.
c Suggest **three** different groups of village people affected by the closures listed in the table. Explain why.
d Choose **two** issues mentioned in the headlines. For each explain how different groups of people would benefit and suffer.

3.7 A village changes...

Where is Leire?

A

Leire is a village in south Leicestershire. Since the 1950s counter-urbanization has seen many families move into the village. Some have moved into old houses; others into newly-built small estates. This has caused the community to change.

1 Study **Source A**.
   a   Describe the location of Leire.
   b   Suggest groups of people who would benefit from living in this location. Explain your choices.

2 Study **Sources B** and **C**.
   a   From which direction was the photograph taken?
   b   On an outline sketch of the village use colours to shade:
      • the fields, gardens, trees and other open spaces
      • the roads
      • the disused railway
      • housing and other uses of buildings.
   c   Label or add symbols to identify housing of different ages using the key in **Source C**.

3   a   Use **Source D** to draw a graph that shows the growth in population and housing from 1891- 2001 (est).
   b   What was the population increase from 1961 to 1991? How has this changed since the 1991 census?
   c   Find evidence that housing growth has continued since the photo was taken in 1995.

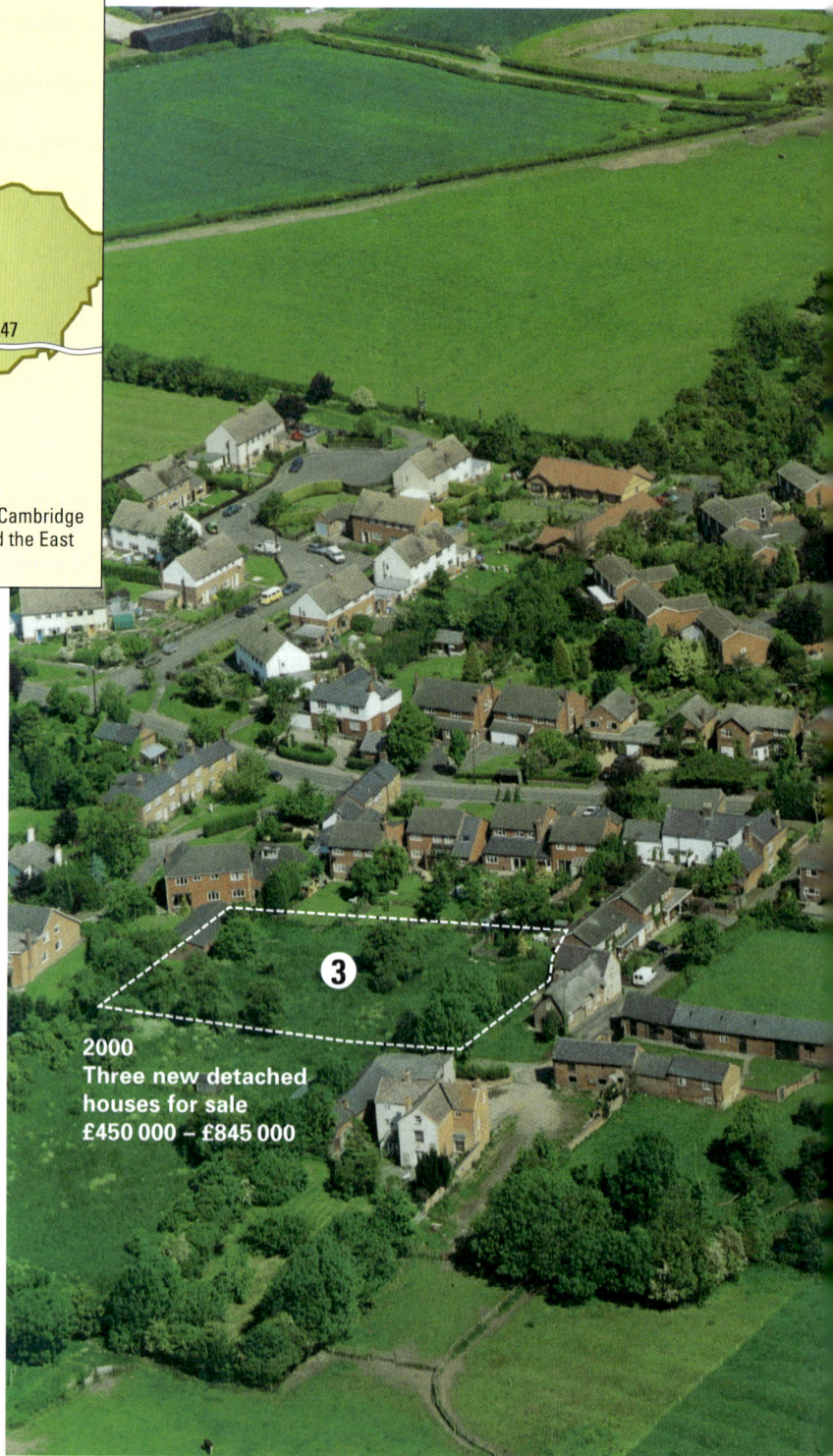

3

**2000
Three new detached houses for sale
£450 000 – £845 000**

4   The parish council has asked you to write a short article on 'The growth in village housing since 1950'. Refer to distance, direction, housing layout, age and types in your article. You may include a maximum of two illustrations.

Aerial photograph of Leire taken in 1995

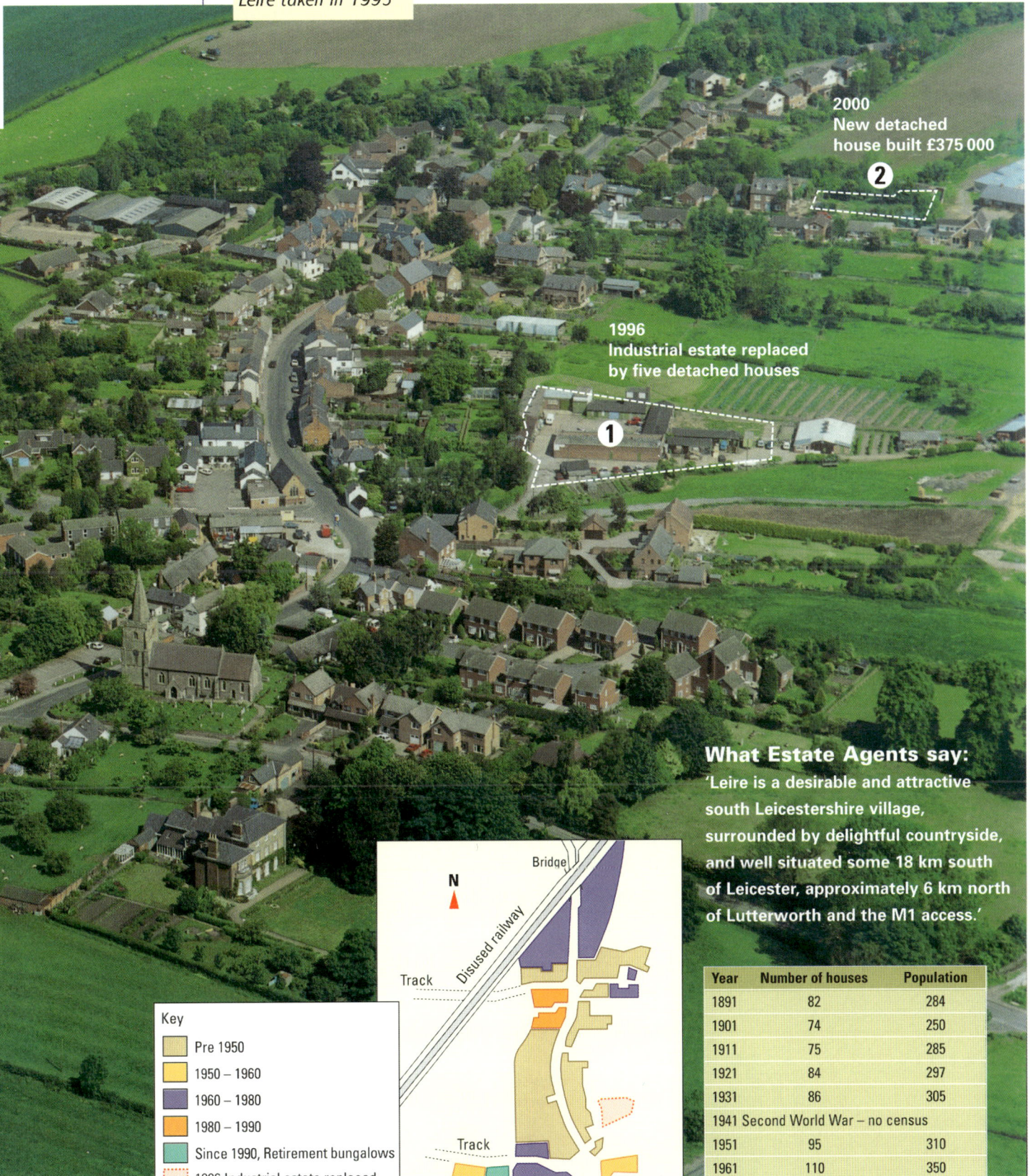

2000
New detached
house built £375 000
2

1996
Industrial estate replaced
by five detached houses
1

What Estate Agents say:
'Leire is a desirable and attractive
south Leicestershire village,
surrounded by delightful countryside,
and well situated some 18 km south
of Leicester, approximately 6 km north
of Lutterworth and the M1 access.'

Bridge

N

Track

Disused railway

Track

Key

- Pre 1950
- 1950 – 1960
- 1960 – 1980
- 1980 – 1990
- Since 1990, Retirement bungalows
- 1996 Industrial estate replaced by detached housing
- Since 2000 Executive detached houses

0   250   500 metres

C

Growth of housing in Leire up to 2000

Year	Number of houses	Population
1891	82	284
1901	74	250
1911	75	285
1921	84	297
1931	86	305
1941 Second World War – no census		
1951	95	310
1961	110	350
1971	130	420
1981	180	430
1991	201	535
2001(est.)	216	563

D *More people mean more houses*

3.8

... for better or worse?

From farming village to commuter village

If you live in a town or city many services are taken for granted. Shops, a doctor's surgery and public transport are easily accessible. In some villages, however, access to these services is becoming more difficult. In Leire the self-sufficient rural community of 100 years ago is being replaced by those who can afford to travel elsewhere for amenities and services using cars. Although they wish to live in rural areas they do not create enough local demand to keep village services open. Closure makes it difficult for the traditional villagers to continue to live a sustainable way of life without a car. The changes affecting Leire are typical of many villages close to urban centres in the UK.

A

A self-sufficient community – employment in 1891

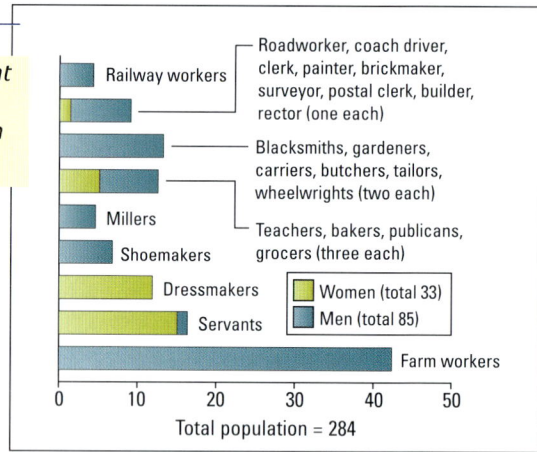

Railway workers

Roadworker, coach driver, clerk, painter, brickmaker, surveyor, postal clerk, builder, rector (one each)

Blacksmiths, gardeners, carriers, butchers, tailors, wheelwrights (two each)

Millers

Shoemakers

Teachers, bakers, publicans, grocers (three each)

Dressmakers

Women (total 33)

Servants

Men (total 85)

Farm workers

Total population = 284

B

*Employment structure, by **social class**, 1991*

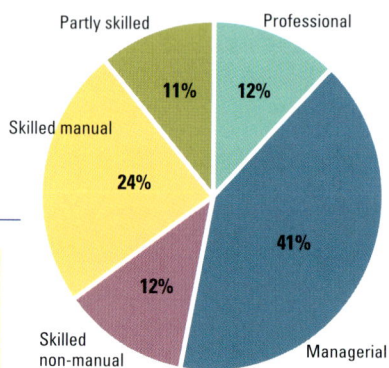

Partly skilled 11%
Professional 12%
Skilled manual 24%
Managerial 41%
Skilled non-manual 12%

Property and car ownership, 1991

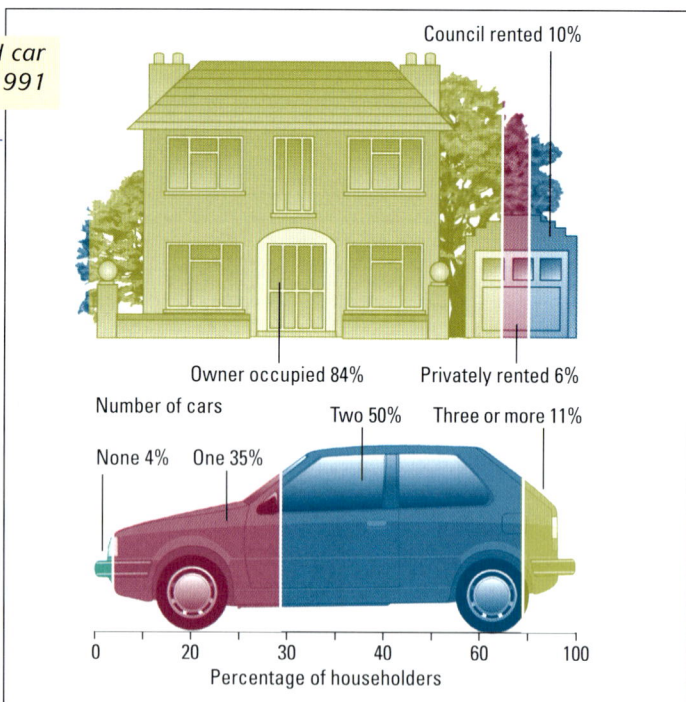

C

Council rented 10%

Owner occupied 84%

Privately rented 6%

Number of cars

Two 50%   Three or more 11%

None 4%   One 35%

Percentage of householders

Age-sex structure, 1991

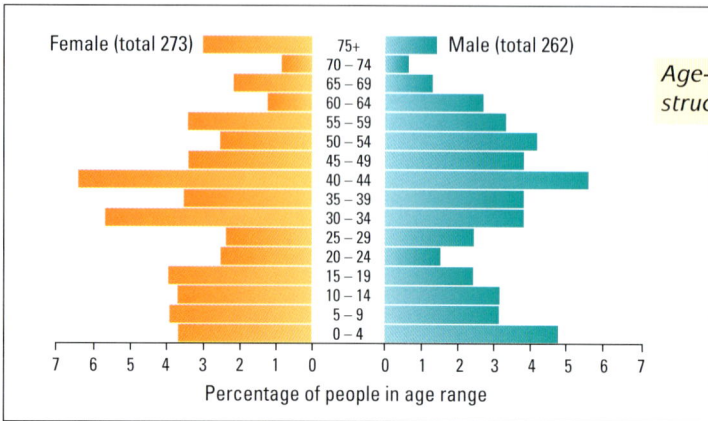

D

Female (total 273)   Male (total 262)

Percentage of people in age range

1 Study **Sources A** and **B**.
a Which **two** types of work were most common in 1891?
b Make two lists:
  • jobs mostly done by men
  • jobs mostly done by women.
c Comment on this division of labour. How different might it be today?
d What type of jobs did the villagers do in 1991? Compare this with 1891.

2 Study **Source C**. How might your answer to question 1d explain the patterns of:
• housing tenure
• car ownership?

3 Study **Source D** then write down the **true** statements from those given below:
• *There were more males than females living in Leire in 1991.*
• *In 1991, more than one-third of the population was aged 30-49.*
• *Approximately 30% of the population was aged 10-19.*
• *There was a higher percentage of females than males aged 65 +.*
• *In 1991, there was a low percentage of people aged 20-29 in the village.*

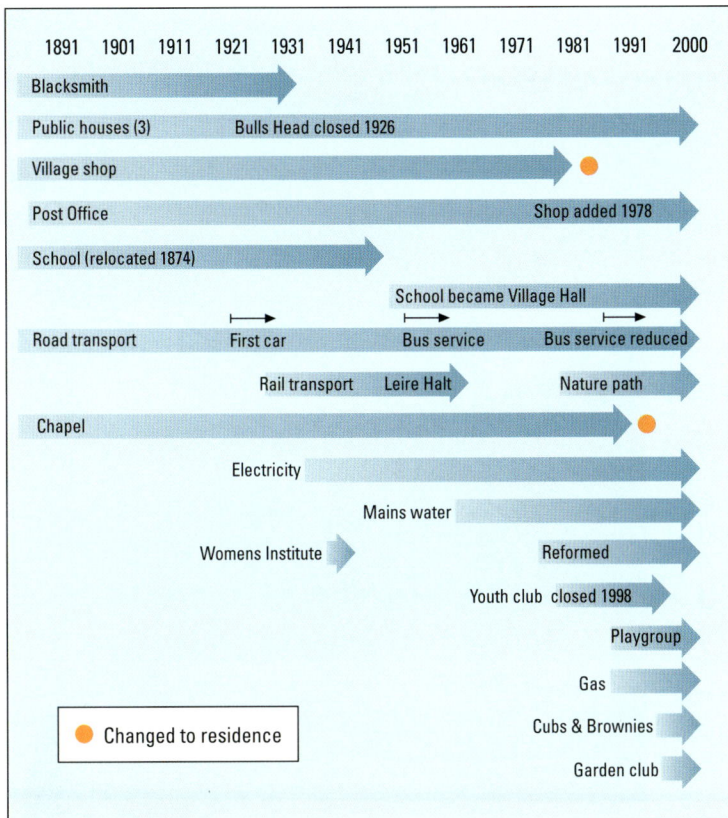

Source E — Changing services, 1891-2000

	1891	1901	1911	1921	1931	1941	1951	1961	1971	1981	1991	2000
Blacksmith	■■■■■■■■■■■■■▶											
Public houses (3)	■■■■ Bulls Head closed 1926 ■■■■■■■■■■■■■▶											
Village shop	■■■■■■■■■■■■■■■■■ ●											
Post Office	■■■■■■■■■■■■■ Shop added 1978 ■■■▶											
School (relocated 1874)	■■■■■■■■■■■■▶											
School became Village Hall						■■■■■■■■■■▶						
Road transport	■■■ First car ■■■ Bus service ■■ Bus service reduced ■■▶											
Rail transport	■■■ Leire Halt ■■■■ Nature path ■■▶											
Chapel	■■■■■■■■■■■■■■■■■ ●											
Electricity	■■■■■■■■■■■■■■■■▶											
Mains water	■■■■■■■■■■■■▶											
Womens Institute	■■■▶ Reformed ■■■■▶											
Youth club closed 1998	■■■■■■■■▶											
Playgroup	■■■■▶											
Gas	■■■▶											
Cubs & Brownies	■■▶											
Garden club	■▶											

● Changed to residence

F A few local difficulties...

Getting up early to catch the school bus. The parents club together to pay for a minibus to take their children to primary schools. Buses are provided to take secondary children to their school.

Local Guide Hours of opening

	Mon, Tues, Thurs, Fri	Weds	Sat	Sun
Post Office	9.00–1.00/2.00–5.30	9.00–1.00	9.00–12.30	Closed
Shop	Mon–Sat As P.O. plus 6.45–7.30am			9.00–12.30

	Mon to Fri	Sat	Sun
Garage	8.00–5.30	8.00–12.30	Closed
Pubs	Mon to Sat 12.00–2.30/5.30–11.00		Sun 12.00–10.30

Buying essential items can be difficult

Wood's Coaches — Mondays to Saturdays only

Rugby	–	0900	1100	1300	1500	1730
Leire	0721	0958	1158	1358	1558	1831
Leicester	0831	1048	1248	1448	1650	1918
Leicester	0650	0905	1105	1305	1535	1725
Leire	0737	0952	1152	1352	1622	1823
Rugby	0828	1043	1243	1443	1713	–

Catching a bus can be difficult

SOLD Daisy Cottage was the cheapest house sold in Leire in 1995 at £53 750. Since then no other house has been sold below £99 000.

To Rent LEIRE...£475pcm Large, 3 bed semi, fully furnished, lounge, dining, kitchen, bathroom. Garage, off-road parking

Buying or renting an affordable house can be difficult

4 Study **Source E**.
a List **three** services which have been closed or reduced since 1891.
b Suggest why some services are no longer present.
c List **three** services and activities that have been added to the village since 1981. Suggest why.
d Suggest how **four** of these changes may have affected the quality of life for different groups of people.

5 Study the local difficulties shown in **Source F**.
a What problems exist for the following groups of people?
• a working couple with children of primary school age
• a home-worker who needs to buy a stamp on Wednesday at 3 p.m.
• two teenagers who want to spend Saturday evening in Leicester
• a young couple who wish to buy or rent their first house in Leire.
b Suggest other situations that this service provision makes difficult.

6 Read the proposals made by the government in **Source G**.
a What is meant by '...to sustain village life...'?
b Suggest how **three** of these proposals could solve some of the problems facing villagers in Leire.

7 Leire's parish council is developing its own village website. Local businesses will fund it by advertising on the site. The site already contains your article on the history of housing and the Rural White Paper proposals for villagers to email comments. What else do you think the website should contain and why?

Source G

In November 2000, the government produced a **Rural White Paper**. The proposals try to make it easier to sustain village life in rural areas. They include:

• rural shops, garages, post offices to pay less tax
• tax increases for owners of second homes; local people to get preference on house sales
• parish councils can apply for grants of £10 000 to fund a car for village use
• post offices to become one-stop shops with computer technology and banking facilities
• 50% of rural dwellers to live within a ten minute walk of an hourly bus service
• voluntary groups can apply to a Community Service Fund to provide any village service
• planning permission to build executive houses only to be given if the same number of cheap, affordable houses for rent or sale are built by the builders
• £30 million to increase policing
• each police station to have a drugs worker to reduce drugs-related crime

G A White Paper for a green countryside – nine solutions for sustainable living

Too many townies?

Parks for the people

National Parks have been created in England and Wales since 1951. There are two main reasons:
- some areas of outstanding natural beauty needed protection from urban sprawl
- increased car ownership gave greater access from urban areas causing traffic problems and conflicts with people living in the rural areas.

The Lake District is a National Park. The Lake District National Park Planning Board was set up to manage conflict between local people, the environment and visitors. It is also responsible for planning in the Park. Its aim is to ensure that land use is managed so that it is sustainable and can be enjoyed by future generations. The fourteen million visitors per year, many from urban areas, create many problems in this rural area. Two of these problems are footpath erosion and traffic congestion.

The Langdale Valley – a honeypot site **A**

Some areas, such as the Langdale Valley, attract more visitors than others. It attracts people because of its beauty and ease of access from Ambleside and Windermere. In **honeypot sites** such as this, careful thought is given to strategies that balance the different conflicts.

An eroded footpath in Stickle Ghyll, 1970s **B**

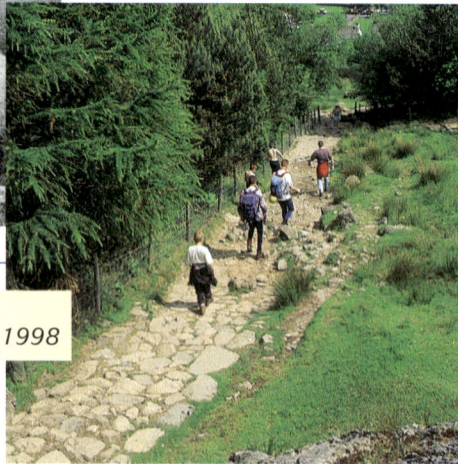

The same footpath in 1998 **C**

What is footpath erosion? **D**

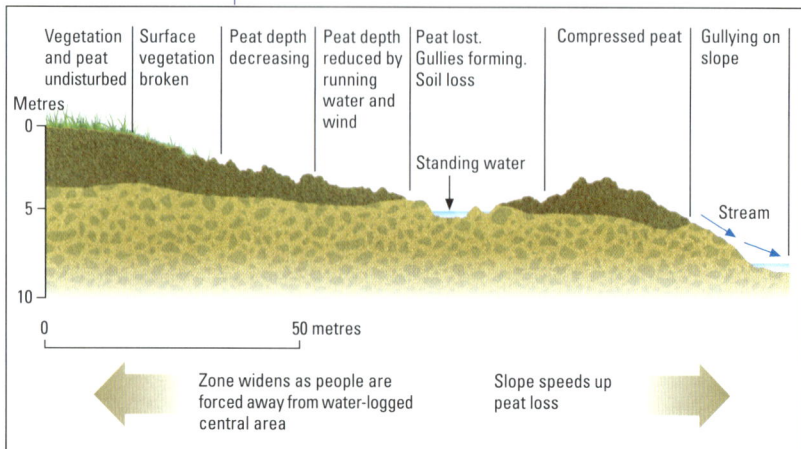

| Vegetation and peat undisturbed | Surface vegetation broken | Peat depth decreasing | Peat depth reduced by running water and wind | Peat lost. Gullies forming. Soil loss | Compressed peat | Gullying on slope |

Metres
0 –
5 –
10 –

Standing water

Stream

0   50 metres

Zone widens as people are forced away from water-logged central area

Slope speeds up peat loss

1 Look at the image on page 41.
  a How many National Parks are there in England and Wales?
  b List the National Parks in order of creation. Which new one may be created in 2002?

2 a Use the image to describe the location of the Lake District National Park.
  b Use an atlas or road map to describe how would you get there by road from your home. Refer to distances, direction, road names and places on your route.

3 Look at **Source A**.
  a Describe the scene.
  b Suggest **three** conflicts that may take place between different groups of people in places such as the Langdale Valley.

4 a Describe the effects of people shown in **Source B**.
  b How has the scene changed in **Source C**?

5 Look at the information in **Source D**.
  a Describe how footpaths get widened by walkers.
  b Explain the consequences of footpath erosion for the environment.

E *A history of footpath protection below Stickle Tarn*

Key

Contour interval 50m

.... New path

········ Right of way

ﾟﾟﾟﾟ Major crags

◆ Point reached by volunteer work parties alone

◆ Top limit of pitched path (1989)

Pavey Ark
Langdale Pikes
▲ 736m
Stickle Tarn
Harrison Stickle
Dam
Stepping stones
Stickle Ghyll
Bridge funded by the friends of the Lake District
Raven Crag
New Dungeon Ghyll Hotel
Ambleside
P   P
Old Dungeon Ghyll Hotel
B5343
N
0   500m

1969:	footpath erosion recognized as a problem
1972:	LDNP wardens shovel scree to form a footpath
1973:	volunteers use experimental techniques to construct a footpath to the west of the Ghyll
Late 1970s:	path built as far as the plateau
Early 1980s:	attempts to make a cobbled path
1982:	full time workers from the Manpower Services Commission's Community Enterprise Scheme take over the work
1983:	bridge built across the Ghyll using a donation from the 'Friends of the Lake District'
1985:	airlift of 700 tonnes of soil and stone to establish vegetation on bare scree
1987:	cobbled path reaches the higher waterfalls

A car park at the foot of Stickle Ghyll

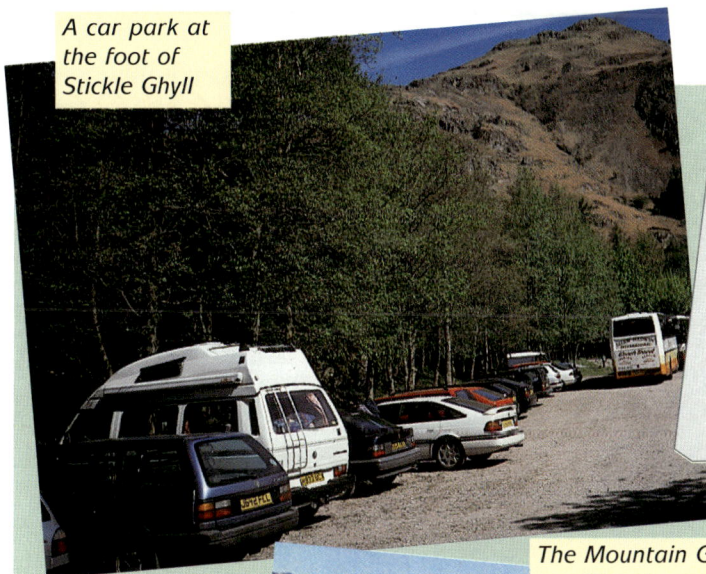

F *National Park's policy 13.5 on traffic and parking*

The National Park Authority's policy on the provision of rural car parks is that they should be provided only where:

- they can be satisfactorily integrated into the landscape
- their use can be related to the capacity of the area
- they are designed to provide access to areas that are managed wholly or partly for recreation, or to give direct access to footpaths, or to provide the most satisfactory solution to an existing parking problem.

The Mountain Goat bus provides a service to remote Lakeland valleys

It is not only footpaths that suffer badly from visitor pressure. The roads that lead into the Langdale Valley can be heavily congested especially in summer.

6 Study **Source E**.

a Describe the changes which have taken place on the footpath below Stickle Tarn since 1969.

b Suggest how these changes could have positive and negative effects on the environment.

7 a The car park shown in **Source F** is at grid reference 295064. (See OS map extract on page 60.) Assess this car park according to the National Park's 13.5 policy on traffic and parking.

b In what ways could the Mountain Goat bus reduce traffic congestion in the Langdale Valley?

3.10 The Langdale Valley – a place to play?

Key

P Parking

Λ Camping

National Trust property

.... Footpath

.... Bridleway

Contours are at 10 metre vertical intervals

Secondary road

Lake District National Park Authority

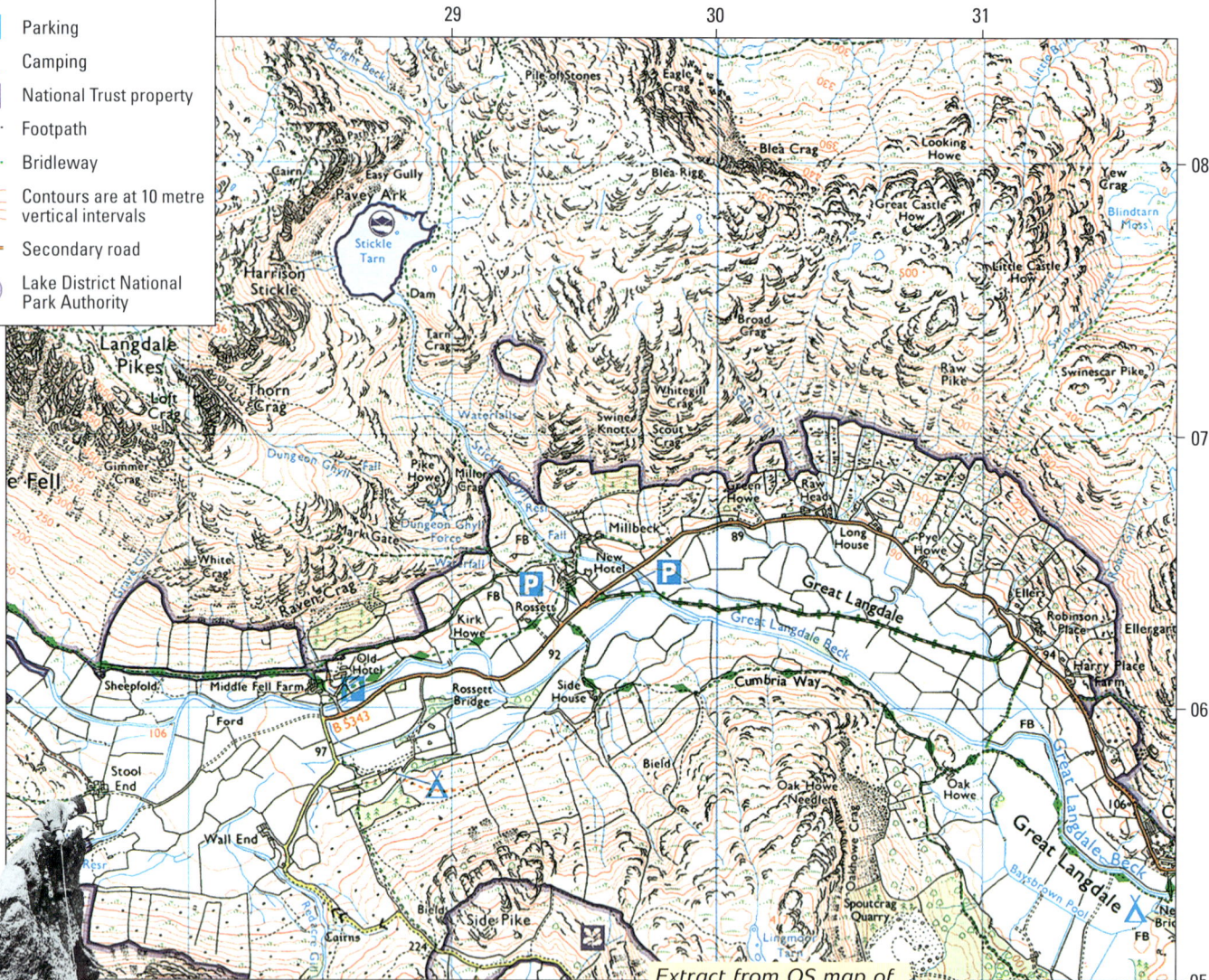

Extract from OS map of the Langdale Valley
1:25000 4cm = 1km

© Crown Copyright 1998

A

The spectacular landforms and scenery of the Lake District and other glaciated areas have attracted visitors for many years. Some have come to walk or climb on the mountains; others use the lakes for leisure; many just holiday on the floor of the valleys. Although being a National Park gives the area some protection, visitor pressure on all parts of the glaciated landscape is causing concern and conflict.

Victorian climbers

1 Study **Sources A** and **B**.

a Label an outline copy of **Source B** with the following locations:
  • Great Langdale Beck
  • Pavey Ark
  • Stickle Tarn.

b Annotate each location with a reason why they are attractive to visitors.

c From the map in **Source A**, add to your copy other locations of natural features that would interest visitors. Annotate each to show why they are attractive.

2 a Give a six-figure grid reference for each of the photo locations in **Source C**.

b Suggest some advantages that the visitors bring to local people.

B

Aerial photo of the Langdale Valley

Old Dungeon Ghyll hotel

New Dungeon Ghyll hotel

Campsite beside Langdale Beck

3 Produce a brochure, a TV or radio script, or a website page designed to advertise the Langdale valley and attract more visitors. Before you start, be clear about the age and interests of the different groups of people you are trying to attract.

Visitor accommodation provides additional or alternative income and work for people living in or near the Langdale Valley

C

3 If I had a coastline ...

The global population continues to grow at an alarming rate. Over 6000 million people were in need of food, water, shelter and employment at the start of the twenty-first century. Where can they all live?

Although people are migrating away from urban areas in MEDCs, many people, especially in LEDCs, regard leaving rural areas for the city as essential for their survival although many end up in squatter settlements. Countries with sufficient wealth and a coastline have produced some imaginative ideas to solve the pressures of providing housing and services in a limited space.

As an island nation with limited space, land prices are now so high in Japan that it makes sense to invest in building cities out to sea. Engineers are designing giant floating platforms several kilometres long. They will be moored over a kilometre offshore and connected to the coast by road and rail bridges. As well as housing, the platforms will be used as airports, harbours and holiday islands for water sports enthusiasts. This idea will also reduce earthquake damage in Japan. The platforms can also be extended, moved and even hired by another country if the population falls! The first full-scale demonstration of an airstrip was unveiled in August 2000.

Japan's Mega-Float solution

A

Breakwater

Floating structure

Bridge

Seabed

B *Cities on the sea*

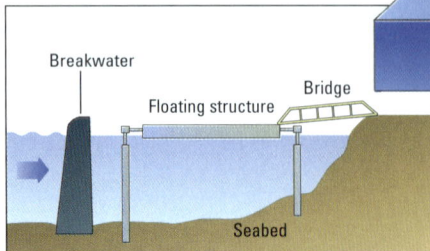

C *Megalopolis 2015*

City	Population (millions)	Country	LEDC/MEDC	Coastline
Tokyo	28.7	Japan	MEDC	Yes
Mumbai (Bombay)	27.4	India	LEDC	
Lagos	24.4	Nigeria		
Shanghai	23.4			
Jakarta	21.2			
São Paulo	20.8			
Karachi	20.6			
Peking	19.4			
Dhaka	19.0			
Mexico City	18.8			

Source: Global Report on Human Settlements

1 Study **Sources A** and **B**.
  a What problems does Japan need to solve?
  b How might the Mega-Float solution solve these problems?
  c Suggest some disadvantages of living on a floating platform.

2 Study **Source C**.
  a Use an atlas to help you complete a copy of the table.
  b Choose **one** LEDC city and **one** MEDC city from this table. Find out how each has tried to solve problems caused by rapid urbanization.

Glossary

Term	Definition	Page
Asylum seeker	A person who applies to live in a new country to avoid persecution in the country they are trying to leave.	47
Census data	The information gained from an official population count.	21
CBD	The Central Business District is the main commercial and shopping area of a city.	20
Colony	A country that has been taken over and ruled by another country.	23
Community	A group of people usually living in the same area who share a common origin, culture or religion.	6
Commuter	Someone who lives some distance from the workplace and who travels daily to and from work.	18
Comprehensive redevelopment	A housing policy which involves the clearing of areas of low-quality buildings and their replacement with a new, higher-quality environment.	16
Conurbations	Large urban areas that are created by the growth and merging of a number of smaller urban areas.	52
Council housing	A type of housing tenure where the houses are owned by local government and are rented to the people who live in them.	12
Counter-urbanization	The process by which an increasing number of people within a country live in the countryside as opposed to towns and cities. This could be the result of natural increase and/or migration.	52
Economic migrant	A person who moves to another place in the hope of gaining a higher standard of living.	46
Gridlock	A situation on the roads where there are so many vehicles that all traffic movement stops.	18
High order goods	Items which are bought infrequently and are often expensive. They are sometimes called comparison goods.	20
High range	Goods or services have a high range when people are prepared to travel long distances to reach them. This usually applies to high order goods.	21
Honeypot site	An attractive place where, because of its popularity, environmental damage may be caused by excessive use.	58
Housing tenure	The conditions under which a household inhabits its home. Common forms of housing tenure include owner occupied, privately rented, and council rented.	8
Indicators of development	Those factors which can be measured to show the degree of development of a country or region.	7
Infant mortality	The number of deaths per 1000 live births of children before their second birthday. Infant mortality is often used as an indicator of development for a country or region.	22
Industrial Revolution	The period of time in a country or region's development when it changes from being mainly a rural agricultural society with small scale 'cottage' industries to one which is based on large scale manufacturing industry in urban areas.	11
Inner city	The zone surrounding the CBD in a city. Although traditionally areas of low-quality housing in MEDCs, these are areas of rapid change and development	12
Labour intensive	Industries which rely on people rather than machines to provide the effort to produce their goods or deliver their services.	11
Low order goods	Items which are bought frequently and which are usually cheap. They are sometimes called convenience goods.	20
Low range	Goods or services have a low range when people are prepared to travel only short distances to reach them. This usually applies to low order goods.	20
Metropolis	A single settlement of outstanding size and importance. It is often the capital city of a country e.g. London, Paris.	23
Migrants	People who move from one place to live in another.	42
Migration	The process of moving from one place to live permanently or semi-permanently in another.	24
Neighbourhood	The area surrounding a person's home and containing many of the services important to that person. A neighbourhood will have definite boundaries.	6
Non Government Organizations (NGOs)	Groups of people who work with communities in order to improve their quality of life. They are separate from official local and national agencies but sometimes work with them. Most of their work is in LEDCs.	25
Perception	A person's image of an area. Perceptions are often based on second hand information and may be quite different from reality.	7
Private sector	Any industry – primary, secondary or tertiary – that is owned and managed by private individuals or companies.	50
Public sector	Any industry – primary, secondary or tertiary – that is owned and managed by local and national governments.	50
Quality of life	The happiness, well-being and satisfaction of a person. Among the many factors that influence quality of life are the person's family, income and access to services.	7

Refugees People who move, usually to another country, in order to escape religious or political persecution or other life-threatening situations. Asylum seekers are refugees. *46*

Rural White Paper A government proposal that should provide for sustainable development in the countryside. *57*

Self-sufficient A situation where a person or a community provides all basic needs without having to trade with groups outside that community. *48*

Shiv Sena/BJP A grouping of Indian political parties who united to form a government. *27*

Social class A way of distinguishing groups of people in society by some or all of the following indicators – inherited or acquired wealth, education, attitudes, language, behaviour. *56*

Social housing Where access to the type of housing tenure is based upon individual or community needs. *34*

Social segregation The process by which people having different incomes, and coming from different socio-economic groups, become separated and live apart from each other. *11*

Standard of living Those factors which affect a person's quality of life and which can be measured. Many measures of a person's standard of living are to do with possessions. *7*

Suburbs The area found towards the edge of the city and beyond the inner city. In MEDCs the suburbs usually have low-density housing and can be divided into the inner and outer suburbs. *12*

Sustainable Capable of being maintained over time for future generations to use or enjoy. *45*

United Nations An organization made up of delegates from almost all countries of the world. The UN headquarters are in New York and it debates issues of global development. *22*

Urbanization The process by which an increasing number of people live in towns and cities as opposed to the countryside. This could be the result of natural increase and/or migration. *42*

Urban dereliction The neglect and decay of parts of a town or city. *34*

Urban renewal The process whereby the derelict areas of a town or city are improved by upgrading existing buildings. This process is sometimes known as gentrification. *14*

Urban-rural fringe The areas on the very edge of a town or city where it meets the countryside. *18*

Values and attitudes Values are the feelings and beliefs that people hold. Attitudes are the expressions of those values in the lives and actions of people. *6*